GRADE

TEACHING SELF-REGULATION

75 INSTRUCTIONAL ACTIVITIES TO FOSTER INDEPENDENT, PROACTIVE STUDENTS

AMY S. GAUMER ERICKSON
PATRICIA M. NOONAN

Solution Tree | Press

a division of
Solution Tree

555 North Morton Street
Bloomington, IN 47404
800.733.6786 (toll free) / 812.336.7700
FAX: 812.336.7790

email: info@SolutionTree.com
SolutionTree.com

Visit **go.SolutionTree.com/SEL** to download the free reproducibles in this book.

Printed in the United States of America

Library of Congress Cataloging-in-Publication Data

Names: Erickson, Amy S. Gaumer, author. | Noonan, Patricia M., author.

Title: Teaching self-regulation : seventy-five instructional activities to foster independent, proactive students, grades 6-12 / Amy S. Gaumer Erickson, Patricia M. Noonan.

Description: Bloomington : Solution Tree Press, [2022] | Includes bibliographical references and index.

Identifiers: LCCN 2021044105 (print) | LCCN 2021044106 (ebook) | ISBN 9781951075774 (paperback) | ISBN 9781951075781 (ebook)

Subjects: LCSH: Learning, Psychology of. | Student-centered learning. | Affective education. | Educational psychology.

Classification: LCC LB1060 .E73 2022 (print) | LCC LB1060 (ebook) | DDC 370.15/23--dc23/eng/20211018

LC record available at https://lccn.loc.gov/2021044105

LC ebook record available at https://lccn.loc.gov/2021044106

Solution Tree

Jeffrey C. Jones, CEO
Edmund M. Ackerman, President

Solution Tree Press

President and Publisher: Douglas M. Rife
Associate Publisher: Sarah Payne-Mills
Art Director: Rian Anderson
Managing Production Editor: Kendra Slayton
Copy Chief: Jessi Finn
Senior Production Editor: Suzanne Kraszewski
Content Development Specialist: Amy Rubenstein
Copy Editor: Kate St. Ives
Proofreader: Mark Hain
Cover Designer: Rian Anderson
Editorial Assistants: Sarah Ludwig and Elijah Oates

ACKNOWLEDGMENTS

We would like to thank the thousands of educators, families, and students with whom we have had the pleasure to work over the past two decades. Examples in this book originated from professional development projects conducted in multiple states, including Arizona, Kansas, Missouri, and Texas. Educators' commitment to developing socially and emotionally engaged, career-equipped, lifelong learners continues to impress and inspire us. Day after day, secondary educators go above and beyond their job descriptions to meet the intrapersonal, interpersonal, and cognitive needs of middle and high school students through their personal dedication, pursuit of continuous improvement, and unflinching faith in the capacity of students.

This book would not have been possible without the dedication and contributions of colleagues and staff who condensed thousands of research studies into easy-to-understand segments that enable educators to expand their professional knowledge through concise and poignant research. The research was then applied, supporting the development of a schoolwide professional learning series as well as the instructional activities within this book.

Finally, we would like to thank our families. This book represents weeks on the road, nights and weekends lost in our own thoughts, and two decades of dedication to educational research. Their unfailing belief in the meaningfulness of the work and our capacity to support educators to continually improve helped us have the self-efficacy, self-regulation, and assertiveness to make this book a reality.

Solution Tree Press would like to thank the following reviewers:

Randy Barker
CTE CS Teacher
Cedar Valley High School
Eagle Mountain, Utah

Louis Lim
Vice-Principal
Richmond Green Secondary School
Richmond Hill, Ontario, Canada

Visit **go.SolutionTree.com/SEL** to download
the free reproducibles in this book.

TABLE OF CONTENTS

Reproducibles are in italics

ABOUT THE AUTHORS

Amy S. Gaumer Erickson, PhD, is an associate research professor at the University of Kansas. Her work focuses on the implementation of evidence-based instructional practices within a multitier system of supports (MTSS) that empower students to become socially and emotionally engaged, career-equipped, lifelong learners. Through her collaboration with state departments of education, Dr. Gaumer Erickson designs high-quality professional learning and implements evaluations that track the fidelity of implementation, as well as the short-term, intermediate, and long-term outcomes and impacts. Dr. Gaumer Erickson has taught at the middle and high school levels and within urban, suburban, charter, and alternative schools. She also has a passion for rural schools, growing up in a farming community of 1,500 people. Dr. Gaumer Erickson has published numerous articles, more than thirty measures, and four books, and she has been providing high-quality professional development to thousands of secondary-level educators since 2003, learning from these educators through a practice-based research approach.

Visit http://cccframework.org to learn more about Dr. Gaumer Erickson's work.

Patricia M. Noonan, PhD, is an associate research professor at the University of Kansas where she centers her work on providing and evaluating professional development related to improving education for all students. She holds a firm belief in the capacity of students with and without disabilities to achieve positive post-school outcomes through college and career readiness. Much of her work entails providing schoolwide professional development and coaching to trainers, leadership, instructional coaches, and educators while working in close collaboration with state departments of education. Her research often focuses on measuring collaboration, then using the results to improve teaming—a critical yet elusive component of educational improvement. To this end, she has published three books, numerous articles, and an integrated framework, all of which translate research results into practical applications. Throughout this process, Dr. Noonan continually improves her interactive, adaptive professional development practices in both virtual and face-to-face settings.

Visit http://cccframework.org to learn more about Dr. Noonan's work.

To book Amy S. Gaumer Erickson or Patricia M. Noonan for professional development, contact pd@SolutionTree.com.

INTRODUCTION

"Many students don't turn in homework on time, especially larger projects. While I know they have worked on it, they can't seem to get it to me by the due date."

"Students don't take responsibility for themselves. They blame everything and everyone else around them."

"My students refuse to plan. They expect it all to be done for them and still can't get through the steps."

"Some of my students just give up and don't even try when they have a challenging assignment."

These are some common concerns we hear from middle and high school educators across the United States. If you have similar concerns about your students, you are not alone. While self-regulation is integral to in-school and post-secondary success, many of our students struggle to demonstrate self-regulation consistently. The purpose of this book is to support secondary educators in teaching self-regulation through explicit instruction and authentic practice. This timely book provides seventy-five instructional activities to teach self-regulation in any secondary classroom. Throughout the book, we've included quotes and vignettes from real people to illustrate how educators and students engage with the instructional activities.

Why Teach Self-Regulation?

Self-regulation refers to a proactive, self-directed process for attaining goals, learning skills, managing emotional reactions, and accomplishing tasks. For adults and youth, self-regulation can be applied to mastering a skill, focusing on a specific task while avoiding distractions, completing quality work on time, sustaining focus on a goal across years, and implementing self-care and self-calming behaviors.

WHAT TEACHERS SAY

"[After teaching self-regulation] students are actually thinking more in depth about their choices. [Discipline] referrals have decreased in numbers."

—*Donna, behavior specialist*

Consider a time when you've tried to eat healthier, exercise more, manage stress, or save money. Consider when you were more successful versus less successful. What made the difference? Likely, when you experienced success, you addressed the four components of self-regulation.

1. Make a *plan* for what you want to accomplish.

2. Immediately *monitor* progress and interference regarding your goal.

3. *Adjust* by implementing specific strategies when things are not going as planned.

4. *Reflect* on what worked and what you can do better next time.

Now consider each component related to a past unrealized goal. Did you have a plan to eat healthier, but your plan lacked specificity? Did you forget to consistently monitor your plan? Did something get you off track, like an illness or an unexpected financial burden? If you weren't successful, it's likely that you didn't address all four components of self-regulation.

With instruction and practice, students can learn and apply the self-directed process of self-regulation to attain both academic and personal goals, learn new skills, manage complex emotions, and accomplish challenging tasks. Research has shown us that self-regulation skills do not simply arise on their own; rather, they must be purposefully learned (Usher & Schunk, 2018).

Self-regulation doesn't just help low-achieving students, those who struggle with certain subjects, or those who display undesirable behaviors. Practicing self-regulation is important for all of us. At some point, we all encounter obstacles or difficulties in achieving a goal or completing a task. By applying the self-regulation process, we are empowered to overcome obstacles and improve at anything we aspire to achieve.

WHAT TEACHERS SAY

"Self-regulation is an integral part of student success as it teaches them how to have autonomy, inside and outside of the classroom. It empowers them to take responsibility for their decisions and goals, which teaches them to manage time, develop self-efficacy, and plan ahead. These are all qualities that will translate into learning experiences that continue throughout their lives."

—*Rachel, social worker*

If our students struggle with self-regulation, we often regulate for them. "Having trouble staying focused? Sit right here and complete your homework." "Don't remember what homework is due? Let me list it out for you." "Lost your worksheet? Here is another copy." Alternatively, we sometimes think that natural consequences teach desired behaviors. "Didn't do your homework? You earned a zero." These common educator responses are missed opportunities to teach students how to self-regulate. When we provide instruction and intentionally create opportunities to guide students' practice, we gradually shift responsibility, working to build the capacity of students to enact their own plans for success.

While self-regulation is an internal, reflective process, we can teach students a set of skills that empowers them to self-regulate. In addition to planning, to help students develop the ability to effectively self-regulate, we also need to teach them to monitor their progress, adjust their efforts if things aren't going according to their original plan, and apply meaningful reflection. Students can expand their abilities to self-regulate through instruction and integration within content-area learning and experiences. Students develop self-regulation skills the same way they develop skills in mathematics or reading—by learning through direct instruction, opportunities for practice, and feedback consistently provided across time.

WHAT TEACHERS SAY

"To me, self-regulation is a mix of self-control, routine, and follow-through. It's a mix of the mind and the physical habits coming together. Self-regulation is ultimately a lifestyle that allows us to reach our big-picture goals."

—Terese, social studies teacher

What Does Self-Regulation Look Like?

When students self-regulate, they apply the four components of self-regulation to numerous situations in order to attain goals, learn skills, manage emotional reactions, and accomplish tasks. Here are a few examples of common things adolescents work to self-regulate.

- Mastering a game
- Getting to school or work on time
- Saving money for a big purchase
- Focusing attention on a task
- Responding calmly when frustrated
- Eating a balanced diet

- Getting homework done
- Exercising regularly
- Completing daily chores
- Finishing school or personal projects

As students learn to expand how and what they self-regulate, they construct an understanding of important concepts and skills that can be applied to numerous contexts, including academics. Consider the sequence of self-regulation knowledge and skill development (Gaumer Erickson & Noonan, 2018) in table I.1. Which of these abilities can you already observe in the majority of your students? Which ones are lacking? If students entered middle or high school demonstrating these behaviors, how would your classroom operate? What would it sound like? Feel like? When educators purposefully teach self-regulation, it impacts not only each student's ability to create plans, monitor learning, and manage distractions, but also the classroom and school as a whole. This sequence of skill development helps educators solidify instruction and observe their students' growth. It is aligned with instructional activities and assessments that are described in this book.

Table I.1: Self-Regulation Developmental Sequence

Level 1: Developing
• Demonstrates the ability to create a simple plan and immediately reflect on the implemented plan
• Describes and chooses simple strategies for self-calming
• Plans for and practices ignoring some distractions during a task, resulting in increased focus

Level 2: Emerging
• Demonstrates the ability to create a plan to accomplish a task or set of tasks
• Identifies ways to get back on track when distracted
• Develops a plan (with teacher guidance) to self-regulate for common challenging situations and emotional reactions
• Describes the importance of self-regulation for current and future achievement
• Predicts how various actions and decisions would affect outcomes

Level 3: Demonstrating
• Defines self-regulation and describes self-regulation components (planning, monitoring, adjusting, and reflecting)
• Explains personal self-regulation strengths and areas for improvement related to specific situations (such as assignments, technology, and social interactions)
• Demonstrates the ability to make increasingly detailed plans to accomplish tasks
• Identifies potential barriers to plan completion using if–then statements
• Monitors progress of efforts over time
• Reflects on success of effort

Level 4: Generalizing

- Independently creates a plan (detailed set of actions) for short- and long-term aspirations, then monitors progress and effort, adjusts as needed, and reflects
- Self-regulates in multiple settings related to various situations (such as long-term projects, personal goals, and career development)
- Reflects on strengths, challenges, efforts, and outcomes related to self-regulation in specific situations
- Identifies connections between self-regulation and other intrapersonal and interpersonal competencies

Source: © 2018 by Amy Gaumer Erickson and Patricia Noonan. Used with permission.

Visit go.SolutionTree.com/SEL for a free reproducible version of this table.

WHAT TEACHERS SAY

"By the time we got to the end of the year, I didn't have to say a word. Students knew. They planned it out. They wrote papers and monitored their progress. And every month those kids had higher and higher scores."

—Vickie, English language arts teacher

Why Teach Self-Regulation in Secondary Education?

As Rick H. Hoyle and Amy L. Dent (2018) write:

> For over a century, leaders in education policy and practice have argued that a primary purpose of formal schooling is teaching students how to learn. This purpose is achieved when students can self-regulate their learning, which transforms the acquisition of knowledge and skills into an active, autonomous process. (p. 49)

This book is designed to support you in teaching middle and high school students the components of self-regulation as well as provide resources for authentic classroom practice with feedback tied to course activities that are already in place. Ongoing practice can be embedded into any course, any extracurricular activity, and any life experience. When all educators in a school facilitate practice in self-regulation, student responsibility becomes ingrained in the school culture.

Students who apply self-regulation strategies perform better in school, as evidenced by both grade point average and standardized state assessments (Zimmerman & Kitsantas, 2014). In fact, Nancy Frey, John Hattie, and Douglas Fisher (2018), through the method of meta-analysis, find that metacognitive strategies "such as planning, monitoring, and regulating the learning process" (p. 14) produce a high effect size of 0.69 with regard to student achievement (Hattie & Zierer, 2018). As Marie C. White and Maria

K. DiBenedetto (2018) note, by seeing the impact of their efforts, students take ownership over their learning and are empowered to direct their actions toward the desired outcome. In a meta-analysis including thirty-eight studies, Tanya Santangelo, Karen R. Harris, and Steve Graham (2016) find that, when applied specifically to the writing process, self-regulation strategies significantly enhance the quality of students' written products, producing a high-weighted-effect size of 1.06. In addition to self-regulation applied to learning, Zorana Ivcevic and Marc Brackett (2014) define emotional regulation as our "capacity to evaluate emotion regulation strategies and to influence one's affective experience and actions in ways that promote goal attainment in emotionally charged situations" (p. 29). These researchers find a significant positive correlation between emotional regulation and grade point average for both middle school and college students. Finally, self-regulation isn't an innate ability; rather, research consistently concludes that self-regulation is a teachable skill (Duckworth, Grant, Loew, Oettingen, & Gollwitzer, 2011; Frey et al., 2018; Usher & Schunk, 2018; Yeager, Dahl, & Dweck, 2018).

One difficulty that teachers often cite is that some students don't have grit; they give up when the work becomes challenging. Self-regulation is directly tied to students' abilities to persevere in sustaining their attention across time, even when they encounter challenges. By applying the self-regulation process, students experience initial success, which leads them to set more challenging goals for themselves. This self-efficacy—the belief that through hard work they can reach their goals—combined with self-regulation leads to perseverance. Students don't automatically persevere, they must believe in their abilities and have the self-regulation skills to maintain focus and progress toward their long-term goals (Gaumer Erickson & Baird, 2019).

WHAT TEACHERS SAY

"I think the biggest benefit for students is that they are taking ownership for their actions. It has improved their ability to see what is causing them to be late turning in assignments or why they might have missing assignments. I feel, by students developing their competency, they are improving their own organization."

—Drew, science teacher

In our work teaching the instructional practices outlined in this book to educators, both teachers and students have observed measurable impacts. Teachers across subject areas have seen positive outcomes, including improved test scores in science, increased engagement with high-quality essays in language arts, increased quality of artwork and engagement in art, and both improved grades and more accurate predictions of the time necessary to complete homework in mathematics. Educators have reported improved learning and more on-time project submissions with a better understanding of historical events in social studies, increased initiative and self-confidence in physical education, and improved course grades in world languages. Special education teachers have observed students with disabilities displaying better organization and time on task. When asked, students said they had more control over their learning and academic success. They talked about feeling less stressed. Students better understood how their actions directly impacted their performance in school, and their engagement, motivation, and learning improved.

How Do We Teach Students to Self-Regulate?

This book provides secondary educators the tools necessary to facilitate students' development of self-regulation by outlining an array of instructional practices, authentic application examples, and formative assessment techniques that can be applied in any classroom or educational experience. These instructional activities and strategies are designed specifically for adolescents. Prior research shows that social-emotional instruction at the middle and high school levels often fails because these interventions do not respect the adolescent's desire for independence, status, and respect (Yeager et al., 2018). Instead of attempting to suppress these desires, our approach empowers youth to gain independence and achieve any aspiration. In doing so, even the most reluctant students increase their ownership and motivation, applying their enhanced agency to all aspects of their lives, including academics.

At this point, you may be thinking about a specific student and wondering, "He clearly needs these skills, but will he buy into the instruction? Will he put in the effort necessary to increase his self-regulation?" We have heard similar questions from hundreds of educators who later tell us that they were surprised at the high levels of student engagement, especially from students who struggle academically. These same teachers describe how high-achieving students were grateful for this instruction because it helped them manage their time and decrease their stress levels. Throughout the book, we have included quotes from educators and students illustrating how diverse learners connect with and apply self-regulation. We encourage you to skim through these quotes and highlight the ones that resonate with you.

Self-regulation, like all intrapersonal and interpersonal competencies, isn't an innate trait; it's a teachable set of skills. The chapters in this book provide numerous instructional activities for thoroughly teaching students the self-regulation process, helping them learn each of the essential components, and creating opportunities for authentic practice within common classroom activities. The instructional activities included in this book have been taught across hundreds of middle and high schools, in specific courses, and school-wide. To reach all students, many schools provide consistent self-regulation instruction during an advisory, mentoring, or homeroom course. Then each educator designs practice opportunities within their academic courses. This creates a schoolwide common understanding of self-regulation and provides students with numerous opportunities to practice and receive feedback on their development. Other schools have divvied up the instructional activities to be utilized across core content courses—the language arts, mathematics, science, and social studies teachers each facilitate different instructional activities, promoting students' development of self-regulation alongside academic learning. Still other schools have used the instructional activities in their entirety as a course curriculum, often in a mandatory success skills course.

To reach schoolwide implementation, it is often beneficial to start with one or a small group of teachers. As you teach, devote a little time each week to providing self-regulation instructional activities, and whenever possible, connect the self-regulation concepts to your course material or assignments (numerous examples are provided in each chapter). Identify differences in student behaviors and learning as a result of self-regulation instruction and talk with others about students' development. While you may be thinking there isn't time, content-area instructors (including mathematics, science, language arts, social studies, business, technical education, health, and others) who have carved out instructional time to teach self-regulation are rewarded with students using class time more effectively, turning in homework on time and of high quality, managing their progress on projects, studying for exams, and supporting each other to succeed. As Theresa, a high school science teacher, told us:

> I spent two days at the beginning of a science project guiding students to plan their own paths to success. Then throughout the project, I devoted class time to guiding students to monitor and adjust their plans, sharing ideas with each other. All but one student, who was out sick for a week, turned in the project on time and earned a C or better. The teacher across the hall only had 50 percent of students submit the project on time. When I asked students what made the difference, they told me that they knew what to do and didn't feel stressed. Using a little class time to teach self-regulation has paid off!

Instead of regulating for students, Theresa coached her students to take ownership over their success through self-regulation. Educators have told us time and time again that they are able to cover more academic content because students are displaying these academic success behaviors.

WHAT TEACHERS SAY

"I was excited to see their responsibility and their problem-solving strategies in regard to taking on a challenging course. I also enjoyed seeing them take control of their success and feel confident of the path they had chosen."

—*Rachel, geometry teacher*

What Will I Find in This Book?

The seventy-five instructional activities within this book come from practice-based research. Through our collaboration with thousands of middle and high school educators, the initial instruction, scenario-based guided learning, and independent practice activities have been tested and refined in diverse classrooms. Each chapter contains a variety of options to make it easy for educators to select activities that can be most effectively incorporated into their context, based on their grade level, content area, student population, or a variety of other factors. In other words, you don't need to use every activity included in this book—choose the ones that will be most useful in helping *your* students reach the learning targets.

Like learning anything else, self-regulation takes practice over time. In addition to purposeful instruction, students need practice in authentic settings to become proficient. Use your specific content area and context to pinpoint ways for students to practice self-regulation. The best way to help students develop self-regulation is by facilitating multiple opportunities for them to practice the components while providing them with constructive feedback and prompts for self-reflection. In each chapter, you'll read about Mrs. Cooper's research project. This vignette describes how one teacher facilitated students' development through ongoing practice, reflection, and feedback. We have also included quotes from real people to illustrate how educators and students engage with the instructional activities. These quotes come directly from educators and students in schools that have implemented self-regulation instruction and practice. They were collected via interviews, professional development evaluations, and student work examples.

This book is designed as a stand-alone toolkit that any educator in a middle or high school can use to improve instructional practices related to self-regulation; however, we encourage you to embark on this journey with other educators. Use the instructional planning form at the end of each chapter to take notes, modify the scenarios to resonate with your students, and contemplate ideas for facilitating students' practice of the concepts. After reading each chapter, discuss your ideas with colleagues and try out a few of the instructional activities with students. Share your successes, and brainstorm solutions to any barriers you encounter. Chapters 1–7 provide instructional activities, scenarios, and performance-based assessments, with each chapter focusing on specific learning targets. The allocation of time for each instructional activity may vary depending on class size and the depth of students' discussion, but in general, most activities require less than fifteen minutes. The epilogue provides a systems perspective for continuous school-wide improvement of implementation and impacts.

Chapters 1–7 follow a structure that describes deliberate teaching and learning methods, organizing instructional activities into three categories which gradually shift the responsibility to the students, building their competence along the way.

1. **Initial instruction:** These activities support students' development of knowledge around critical concepts, make connections to their lives, and build a shared vocabulary to promote discussion of the critical concepts. Select activities that best match the needs and interests of your students to meet the identified goal of instruction. Initial instruction concludes with a check for understanding.

2. **Guided collaborative learning:** By applying critical concepts of self-regulation using vignettes that approximate adolescents' experiences, students are able to engage in the learning and collaborate with peers to explore diverse perspectives in a nonjudgmental environment. Choose activities that will be relatable to your students, or modify the scenarios within the activities to make them applicable. Guided collaborative learning concludes with a situational judgment assessment.

3. **Independent practice with feedback:** After students understand the concepts of self-regulation, practice with feedback is vital for skill development. This practice can be focused on academic, social, emotional, or personal goals. As the teacher, you can facilitate practice for course-specific projects, essays, presentations, test preparation, or academic success in general. You can also guide students to self-regulate progress toward their personal endeavors, such as health, community activism, or mastering a skill. These activities serve as performance-based assessments.

Chapter 1: Understanding Self-Regulation

Through instructional activities 1–13, students will describe self-regulation; identify why it is important in their own lives; articulate the components of self-regulation as plan, monitor, adjust, and reflect; describe the complexity of the self-regulation process; and reflect on their personal strengths and areas for growth related to the self-regulation components.

Chapter 2: Making a Plan

Through instructional activities 14–25, students will differentiate between a goal and a plan; describe a variety of real-life situations in which self-regulation planning is beneficial; determine behaviors, processes, and time-lines for quality, situation-specific planning; and create personalized, detailed plans for reaching their goals.

Chapter 3: Monitoring Your Plan and Progress

Through instructional activities 26–40, students will identify a variety of ways to monitor both progress and actions, determine methods for monitoring actions and progress within situation-specific self-regulation planning, and design effective monitoring techniques for their personal and academic endeavors.

Chapter 4: Adjusting Your Plan

Through instructional activities 41–52, students will acknowledge that everyone faces challenges and will determine options for adjusting efforts in order to maintain progress toward an objective.

Chapter 5: Reflecting on Your Efforts and Outcomes

Through instructional activities 53–64, students will articulate the purpose of reflection, determine reflection methods for a variety of situations, and engage in self-directed reflection throughout the self-regulation process.

Chapter 6: Putting It All Together

Through instructional activities 65–75, students will analyze situations and determine how each component of self-regulation could be addressed, analyze personal self-regulation habits and knowledge, and apply the self-regulation process to their own endeavors.

Chapter 7: Measuring Growth in Self-Regulation

This chapter guides educators in determining methods for assessing students' perceptions, knowledge, skills, application of skills, and outcomes related to self-regulation. It discusses the purposes and uses of these data.

Epilogue and Next Steps

The book wraps up with resources to guide implementation, including instructional criteria and a practice profile that support educators' reflection on instructional design.

Conclusion

Our charge as educators is to meet our students' learning needs. To this end, teachers around the world are embracing social-emotional learning. You may be feeling nervous about providing this instruction—social-emotional learning likely wasn't a focus of your teacher preparation program. We encourage you to try a few of the instructional activities and reflect along the way. These activities were purposefully designed for the adolescent learner and have been found to be highly engaging. We commend your efforts to help your students improve their self-regulation with these evidence-based instructional activities. Through our work with thousands of middle and high school teachers, we have witnessed growth in the ability of students to self-regulate, resulting in increased learning, goal attainment, and prosocial behaviors. Self-regulation fuels adolescents to become socially and emotionally engaged, career-equipped, lifelong learners.

CHAPTER 1

UNDERSTANDING SELF-REGULATION

Self-regulation is a complex internal process associated with metacognition, motivation, behavior, and management of emotional reactions. We self-regulate when we plan, self-evaluate our progress, and continually adjust our course of action for improved outcomes. By practicing self-regulation, we are empowered to evaluate the effectiveness of our efforts, demonstrate responsibility for our actions, and stay motivated toward achieving our goals (Frey et al., 2018; Noonan & Gaumer Erickson, 2018; Schunk & Greene, 2018). Self-regulation provides a process for reflecting on and adjusting the behaviors that impact our learning (Usher & Schunk, 2018). When we consider how well we self-regulate, it's important to identify both strengths and areas requiring additional focus.

WHAT TEACHERS SAY

"I wanted the kids to be able to break that project down and figure out a plan to be able to complete that challenge over the course of the year."

—*Kate, English language arts teacher*

Consider your classroom instructional activities, assignments, and assessments.

- How do you promote students' self-regulation?

- Do you regulate for students by telling them how to study, giving short-term due dates for long-term projects, or providing class time for them to catch up on missing work?

- How could you shift the responsibility to students while providing them with the scaffolding necessary to facilitate success?

Instead of planning and monitoring *for* students, teachers are shifting to coaching students to self-regulate. As a coach, you guide the students, ask them questions, and prompt them to consider their progress, but you do not design the plan for them. Students will develop and improve their self-regulation as they practice planning, monitoring, adjusting, and reflecting with teacher support.

Let's follow along with a teacher as she shifts from regulating for her students to promoting their self-regulation. Mrs. Cooper teaches freshman English, but her process for promoting students' success on a large project can apply to any subject. We will revisit Mrs. Cooper to learn how she applied the concepts in each chapter and see the reactions from her students.

Mrs. Cooper's Research Project

Mrs. Cooper teaches freshman English, and one of her goals is that every student becomes proficient in researching a topic and writing a research paper. Reflecting on past years, approximately half of her students turned in their research papers on time, and more than 10 percent of students risked failing her course, due in large part to incomplete research projects. Her previous strategy was to break down the preparation for the project into manageable steps and determine short-term due dates. She then gave this outline to students and provided some time in class for independent work. Mrs. Cooper monitored each student's progress and met individually with students if they missed two of her short-term due dates. When she met with students, she told them what they needed to do to get back on track.

This year, Mrs. Cooper has decided that she wants students to take more ownership over completion of their research project. First, she hands out the rubric that she will use to grade the research papers. She explains how rubrics work and then describes each indicator. Students reflect on their past research papers, identifying strengths and areas that are harder for them. Students then read the score descriptions on the rubric, and each student marks where he or she would like to score on each indicator. She encourages students to identify moderately challenging goals (indicator descriptions). After class, Mrs. Cooper reviews each student's rubric goals to ensure that the result, should the goals be met, meets the overall mastery level of 80 percent for the research paper. For students with low expectations of themselves, Mrs. Cooper provides specific verbal and written encouragement, persuading them to set more challenging goals for particular rubric indicators.

Mrs. Cooper is encouraged that students are accurately self-assessing their areas of strength and weakness related to the project, and each student now has a clear understanding of the success criteria.

The instructional activities in this chapter are designed to increase students' understanding of self-regulation, including why it is important now and in the future. These activities guide students' self-appraisal through opportunities to reflect on their behaviors, assess their knowledge, and determine their strengths and areas of need when it comes to self-regulation. Instructional activities are categorized as initial instruction, guided collaborative learning, and independent practice with feedback. These instructional activities progress in complexity, leading to increased student responsibility. By the independent practice stage, students will be able to identify their individual strengths and challenges related to self-regulation.

Outline of Instructional Activities

- **Initial Instruction:** Your goal is for students to be able to describe self-regulation and identify why it is important in their own lives.

  - ➤ **Activity 1**—Defining Self-Regulation
  - ➤ **Activity 2**—Connecting Intrapersonal Competencies
  - ➤ **Activity 3**—We Already Self-Regulate
  - ➤ **Activity 4**—Self-Regulation Components
  - ➤ **Activity 5**—Check for Understanding

- **Guided Collaborative Learning:** Your goal is for students to be able to articulate the components of self-regulation and describe the complexity of the self-regulation process.

  - ➤ **Activity 6**—Is This Self-Regulation?
  - ➤ **Activity 7**—Connecting Outcomes and Behaviors
  - ➤ **Activity 8**—Ten Steps to Homework Completion
  - ➤ **Activity 9**—Situational Judgment Assessment

- **Independent Practice With Feedback:** Your goal is for students to reflect on their personal strengths and areas for growth related to the self-regulation components.

  - ➤ **Activity 10**—Assessing Your Self-Regulation
  - ➤ **Activity 11**—Reflecting on Strengths and Challenges
  - ➤ **Activity 12**—Evaluating Your Efforts
  - ➤ **Activity 13**—Journaling for Ongoing Reflection

Initial Instruction

Through these activities, students learn critical self-regulation concepts, make connections to their lives, and build a shared vocabulary. Your goal for these instructional activities is for students to be able to describe self-regulation and identify why it is important in their own lives.

Activity 1: Defining Self-Regulation

Define self-regulation by reading and displaying this definition: "*Self-regulation is a proactive, self-directed process for reaching goals, learning skills, managing emotional reactions, and accomplishing tasks.*" In small groups, ask students to discuss the definition, especially the meaning of the key words *proactive*, *self-directed*, and *process*. Potential prompts include the following.

- What does *proactive* mean? What are some examples of approaching a situation in a proactive manner?

- What does *self-directed* mean? What does it look like when it's happening? What are some self-directed efforts you've made recently?

- What does *process* mean in this context? Why is this an important piece of self-regulation?

Debrief as a large group (for example, *proactive* means planned in advance; *self-directed* means you do it, not someone else; *process* means a systematic series of actions). Then ask students to rewrite the definition in their own words. Students can refer to this definition as they apply their learning within the following activities.

WHAT STUDENTS SAY

"Self-directed means nobody is forcing you or having to babysit your work. It looks like getting your own homework done on time without being reminded. Self-regulation is managing your time and working toward a goal without anyone having to push you along the way."

—Ninth-grade student

Activity 2: Connecting Intrapersonal Competencies

Show students the competency wheel in figure 1.1. Identify self-regulation as an *intrapersonal* competency (an ability within oneself). Explain the importance of intrapersonal skills: strong intrapersonal skills increase your ability to direct your own learning, have confidence in your abilities, and stay on track to reach your goals. This can lead to increased learning, success in your job,

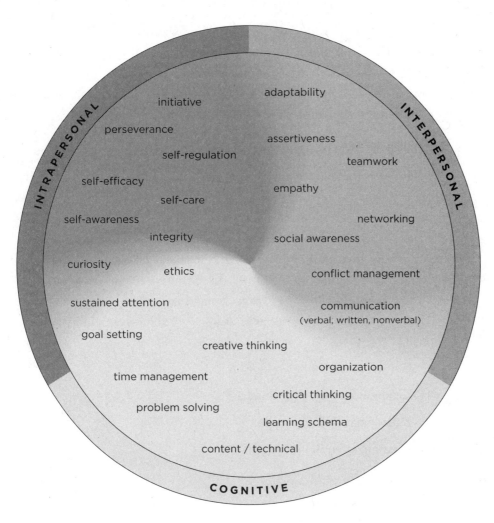

Source: © 2013 by Amy Gaumer Erickson and Patricia Noonan. Used with permission.

FIGURE 1.1: COMPETENCY WHEEL.

Visit **go.SolutionTree.com/SEL** for a free reproducible version of this figure.

better grades, success in college, improved athletic ability, and better health. You will basically improve at anything you aspire to achieve.

Give students a few minutes to look more closely at the competency wheel and identify three competencies they think are related to self-regulation. Encourage students to look up the definitions of terms if needed. Then facilitate a class discussion about which competencies they chose and why, providing additional information or suggestions as necessary. For example, effective *goal setting* helps us ensure that our efforts to self-regulate are directed toward a meaningful, achievable, but still challenging outcome. When we respond to obstacles in our efforts to self-regulate by identifying strategies to overcome the issue (instead of just giving up), we are demonstrating *perseverance*, *adaptability*, and *problem solving*. Additionally, successful self-regulation strengthens our *self-efficacy* by showing us that we can overcome obstacles to make progress toward mastering a skill. Self-regulation also supports *self-awareness* by encouraging us to think more deeply about what we want to accomplish, challenges that we typically encounter, and strategies that support our progress. Within the discussion, note that several competencies simultaneously support successful self-regulation and are themselves, in turn, strengthened by improved self-regulation skills.

Activity 3: We Already Self-Regulate

Explain that there are many things that students already work on self-regulating, even if they don't realize that's what they are doing. Common efforts to self-regulate, for both youth and adults, include exercising regularly and saving money. As a class, ask your students to brainstorm a list of at least ten things that they and their friends have self-regulated in the past or are likely to self-regulate in the future. Keep this list for future reference in activity 11 (page 27), activity 12 (page 28), and activity 24 (page 49). Provide guidance or additional suggestions as necessary. Examples might include the following.

- Getting to school or work on time
- Saving money for a big purchase
- Enhancing skills in a game
- Focusing attention on a task
- Responding calmly when frustrated
- Eating a balanced diet
- Getting homework done
- Exercising regularly
- Completing work tasks on time
- Reading a book
- Speaking kindly to a sibling
- Completing daily chores
- Remembering supplies needed for school
- Finishing school or personal projects
- Managing time spent gaming
- Studying for a test

Next, have students individually list three things that they are already self-regulating successfully and three things that they want to be able to self-regulate more successfully. They can either choose items from the class list or add new items of their own.

"Some of my students came up with some really insightful answers when I asked them how they already use self-regulation in their lives and how they might use it in the future. So that was encouraging, that they know it's going to make a difference in their lives."

—Kate, English language arts teacher

Activity 4: Self-Regulation Components

Show students the self-regulation poster in figure 1.2 (page 20) and apply each of the four components to an example from your own life (for example, eating healthier foods, grading papers in a timely manner, and exercising regularly). Emphasize that all four components are necessary for self-regulation, and provide examples of how missing components (planning poorly, failing to adjust as needed) can cause someone to get off track and fail to meet a goal.

Ask students to think about the components for a minute, reflecting on their individual strengths and weaknesses. Then, associate the four corners of the room with the components listed on the poster (for example, the northwest corner is planning, southwest corner is monitoring, and so on), and have each student stand in the corner for the component that is his or her strength. Staying in those corners, have students discuss why they chose that component as their strength. Ask groups to share some of the ways in which they demonstrate the component. Summarize the discussion by highlighting commonalities and differences across the groups. Display the poster in the classroom for reference during future activities.

"I self-regulate all the time in my own life, and I try to use examples of that with my students—I tell them how I make my plans every day and how I plan throughout my week. I think it really does help for them to be able to relate to what a teacher might do in their everyday lives and not just having to do with school."

—Janelle, algebra 1 and 2 teacher

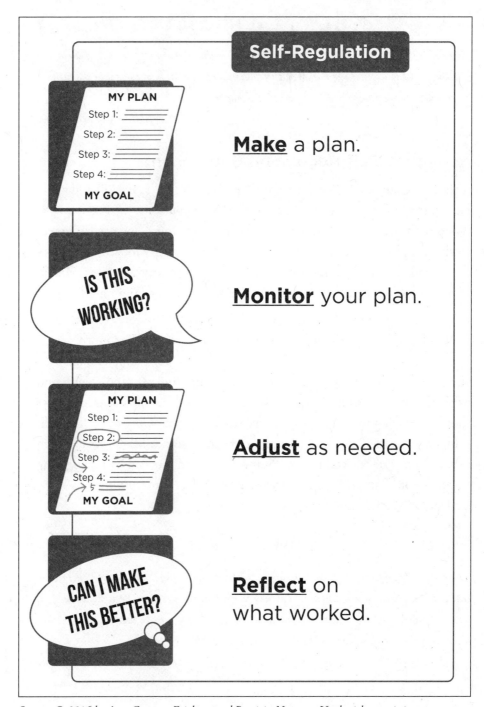

Source: © 2016 by Amy Gaumer Erickson and Patricia Noonan. Used with permission.

FIGURE 1.2: SELF-REGULATION POSTER.

*Visit **go.SolutionTree.com/SEL** for a free reproducible version of this figure.*

Activity 5: Check for Understanding

Using response cards or an online quiz platform, gather individual students' responses to the items displayed in figure 1.3. Review the responses to ensure that students understand the concept of self-regulation. Reteach as necessary. [The answer key for figure 1.3 is: 1–b; 2– false; 3–true; 4–false.]

Understanding Self-Regulation

Multiple Choice

1. Choose the best description of self-regulation.

   a. When you proactively plan for how to reach a goal, learn a skill, or accomplish a task.

   b. When you proactively use a process (such as planning, monitoring the plan, adjusting as needed, and reflecting) to reach a goal, learn a skill, or accomplish a task.

   c. When you follow your teacher's detailed plan (including making changes as suggested by your teacher and reflecting on your progress) for reaching a goal, learning a skill, or accomplishing a task.

   d. When you make progress toward reaching a goal, learning a skill, or accomplishing a task.

True or False

2. _____ Self-regulation is important for academics, but it doesn't really help improve athletic or musical ability.

3. _____ Building your self-regulation skills can also help build your perseverance and improve your goal.

4. _____ You are self-regulating if you check your grades every week.

FIGURE 1.3: CHECK FOR UNDERSTANDING—DEFINITION AND PURPOSE.

*Visit **go.SolutionTree.com/SEL** for a free reproducible version of this figure.*

Guided Collaborative Learning

Scenario-based activities address an array of circumstances to which adolescents can relate. Through these collaborative-learning activities, students gain a deeper understanding of self-regulation concepts. Your goal is for students to be able to articulate the components of self-regulation and describe the complexity of the self-regulation process.

Activity 6: Is This Self-Regulation?

In groups, have students complete figure 1.4 (page 22) to determine if each scenario is an example of self-regulation and explain why or why not. Refer to the definition from activity 1 (page 16) to guide students' analysis of the scenarios.

Scenario	Is this self-regulation? (yes or no)	Why or why not?
Example: Your mom sets a timer and tells you to work on your homework until the timer goes off.	No	It is **not self-directed**—my mom would be driving the effort, not me.
1. You realize that you forgot to study for a test, so you cram five minutes before it starts.		
2. You have a big project that will be due in one month. Your friend says that she's not going to worry about it until next week, so you decide to do the same.		
3. You write down all of the homework that you need to complete and check it off your list as you finish it.		

FIGURE 1.4: IS THIS SELF-REGULATION?

*Visit **go.SolutionTree.com/SEL** for a free reproducible version of this figure.*

Debrief with the whole class. Scenario 1 is not self-regulation because no process was followed—you did not plan in advance. Scenario 2 is not self-regulation because you were relying on someone else to guide your efforts—you were not self-directing your efforts or creating your own plan. Scenario 3 might be self-regulation—you self-directed and proactively planned by writing down your assignment, and then you monitored by checking off completed assignments. This scenario does not provide details about how you might have adjusted your plan or reflected on your efforts, but in general, it follows the definition of self-regulation by being a proactive, self-directed process for accomplishing tasks.

Activity 7: Connecting Outcomes and Behaviors

Explain that even things that seem simple involve a set of actions and considerations. For instance, when trying to avoid being written up at work like in scenario 1 of figure 1.5, it's not enough to say that the person should just return to work on time. Example steps or tasks might include understanding the length of the break and what can be accomplished in that amount of time; estimating time for tasks such as texting, eating a snack, using the restroom, and clocking back in; and setting an alarm for a few minutes before the break is over. Go through the completed example in figure 1.5 with students. Then, in small groups, have students read the scenarios and complete the rest of the table. Encourage them to think creatively; the scenarios do not provide much detail, so students can hypothesize the actions that need to be considered based on their own experience.

Scenario	What is the outcome if the person successfully self-regulates?	What behaviors, thoughts, and actions could the person self-regulate to accomplish the goal?
Example: A friend didn't make the varsity volleyball team her sophomore year.	Making the varsity volleyball team her junior year	• Increase practice to three times a week in the off-season. • Ask friends or coaches to help identify areas for improvement. • Pay attention to nutrition and exercise. • Keep grades up to be eligible to play on the team.
1. Your friend was written up at work for not returning on time after a break.		
2. The voting age is eighteen, and your civic-minded friend will be turning eighteen three months before a big election.		
3. A teammate missed every free throw in her last four games.		
4. Your classmate scored much lower on his SAT (college entrance test) than he had hoped.		
5. A friend was grounded for gaming instead of doing chores.		
6. A classmate in English didn't turn in the writing assignment on time.		
7. You get really stressed before your verbal tests in Spanish class and forget most of the words you've learned.		

FIGURE 1.5: CONNECTING OUTCOMES AND BEHAVIORS.

Visit **go.SolutionTree.com/SEL** *for a free reproducible version of this figure.*

Using a modified jigsaw approach, regroup students into seven expert groups and assign each group to discuss one of the scenarios further, building on the ideas of each person to create a more detailed list of behaviors that the individual could self-regulate to meet his or her goal. Return students to their home group to discuss the additional actions that they identified for their assigned scenarios. Due to class sizes, home groups will likely not address each scenario when they return from their expert groups. This is fine, as the point of this activity is for students to recognize that numerous behaviors likely need to be self-regulated to reach a goal.

WHAT TEACHERS SAY

"When I asked them to think about, 'In the future, how do you think this process might help you?' they came up with things that I didn't think they would come up with. One student talked about self-improvement, which I asked him to clarify. He said, 'You want to learn to play the guitar or you want to work out more, you want to lose weight or you want to learn a different skill like maybe karate or whatever.' The kids have really bought into it, and I even had a couple of kids say they want to use this process to help them save money for college because they don't have anybody and they're worried. They are seeing so many applications for this."

—*Melanie, AVID teacher*

Activity 8: Ten Steps to Homework Completion

Delve a little deeper into scenario 6 in figure 1.5 (page 23): a classmate in English didn't turn in the writing assignment on time. Challenge students to identify ten steps between being assigned the homework and turning it in. Using a shared visual document, work as a whole group to list and order the steps. Reiterate that every time students complete homework and turn it in on time, they are demonstrating self-regulation. Keep the student-generated steps, as we will return to this list in activity 21 (page 44).

Activity 9: Situational Judgment Assessment

Ask students to independently read the scenario and answer the prompt. This scenario extends through each chapter, building on prior answers. A reproducible form with all situational judgment assessments and the corresponding activity numbers is provided in appendix A (page 153).

SCENARIO

In health class, Alex and his classmates learned about the benefits of drinking an adequate amount of water each day. Alex has decided that he does not drink enough water.

Write three questions that Alex should ask himself to become more aware of his water consumption and behaviors that he may need to change in order to meet his goal of drinking an adequate amount of water each day.

Review each student's answers to determine whether the questions they identified would increase self-awareness. Questions might include: How much water do I drink each day? When do I drink water? What do I drink instead of water? How much water should I be drinking each day? Why don't I drink more water (it's not available or I don't like the taste)? Provide specific, constructive feedback to each student.

Independent Practice With Feedback

Through independent practice, students begin applying their learning to their own endeavors. This promotes fluency of the skills and provides opportunities for formative feedback and coaching. Through these instructional activities, your goal is for students to reflect on their personal strengths and areas for growth related to the self-regulation components.

Activity 10: Assessing Your Self-Regulation

The Self-Regulation Questionnaire and Knowledge Test is provided in appendix B (page 157). While this can be copied and completed on paper, it functions more effectively when completed digitally. To administer online, you or your school will need an account on researchcollaborationsurveys.org, a free survey site. Follow the directions on the website to launch the Self-Regulation Questionnaire and Knowledge Test. Through this site, students will receive a summary of their results immediately after completing the assessment, and as the teacher, you will be able to access composite class results, individual summaries, and a complete data file.

WHAT TEACHERS SAY

"I love what the questionnaire tells me about each group of students, but most of all I love the insight it offers each individual student—and so do they!"

—Cindy, high school counselor

Explain to students that they will each take the Self-Regulation Questionnaire and Knowledge Test. Results will help them better understand how they currently self-regulate and measure their knowledge of self-regulation concepts. Assure students that this test will not be used as a grade, but you want them to be reflective and honest because they are going to use the information to think about their strengths and areas for growth.

If you are administering the Self-Regulation Questionnaire and Knowledge Test through the researchcollaborationsurveys.org website, provide students with the survey link and code. If possible, provide the link digitally to save time. Remind students to enter their student-specific number (the school ID) or assign each student a number. This will allow you, as the teacher, to review their individual results. Be sure to remind students that after finishing the test, they should stay on the results page for the next part of this activity.

Tell students that for items 1–28, as they read each item, they should pause for a moment to think about the last couple of months and how well they were able to self-regulate in various situations. For instance, they might consider how often they submitted course assignments on time or how well they accomplished personal goals like saving money, improving in a sport, or learning a new skill. The following are some example items from the survey.

- I plan out projects that I want to complete.

- I keep track of how my projects are going.

- As soon as I see things aren't going right, I want to do something about it.

- I think about how well I've done in the past when I set new goals.

Explain that items 29–49 test knowledge of self-regulation concepts and potential ways to effectively self-regulate in certain situations. Reassure students that there is no expectation that they will know all the right answers yet, because they'll learn more about self-regulation over the next few weeks. Give students adequate time to complete the assessment (ten to fifteen minutes).

After students submit the test, a results page displays automatically. Using these results, ask each student to complete figure 1.6. The self-assessment scores are displayed on a 100-point scale, so they can be interpreted as percentages (similar to the interpretation of grades). The knowledge score is displayed as a total out of twenty items. Students can calculate their percentage correctly by dividing the number of correct answers by 20 and multiplying by 100.

Component	Self-assessed score (from graph)	Rank order components from 1 (highest) to 4 (lowest); if two components have the same score, choose the one that you feel is higher	One item for each component that depicts your strengths	One item for each component that depicts your areas for improvement
Making plans				
Monitoring plans				
Adjusting plans				
Reflecting on what works and what to improve				
	Score	Calculated percentage	One item answered correctly	One item answered incorrectly
My self-regulation knowledge score	/20			

FIGURE 1.6: MY SELF-REGULATION ASSESSMENT RESULTS.

*Visit **go.SolutionTree.com/SEL** for a free reproducible version of this figure.*

Review each student's summarized results and provide feedback and encouragement. For example, if a student's highest component is reflecting and lowest component is planning, you might write, "It's great that you are strong in reflection. This means that you are self-aware. After we practice self-regulation together, you'll have the skills to effectively plan your own success."

Use the teacher view on the website to access both individual and aggregated student results. Log back into your account on http://researchcollaboration surveys.org, scroll to the list of *My Surveys*, locate your survey, and click on the *View* button to open the teacher view for that survey. You'll see an aggregated graph of students' scores on each component and overall, followed by a breakdown of student responses to the self-reflection items. Then you'll see the percentage of students who answered each knowledge item correctly followed by the class average. Review these results and be ready to revisit them as needed to help guide class discussion during activity 11.

WHAT TEACHERS SAY

"I filled out the same questionnaire. I showed the students my questionnaire results, how I answered things, and some things I didn't realize about myself or haven't thought about—I procrastinate."

—*Jill, chemistry teacher*

Activity 11: Reflecting on Strengths and Challenges

Explain to students that they are going to learn how to make plans that are detailed, realistic, and include ways to overcome potential obstacles. When our plans include those things, they are more likely to help us make progress than if we have vague or unrealistic plans. Remind students that the *self* in self-regulation means that we are the ones who must regulate our own actions. Teachers and parents can provide support and help with the learning process, but ultimately self-regulation is a personal ability. Data from over 18,000 students on the Self-Regulation Questionnaire and Knowledge Test (activity 10, page 25) show that the majority of students feel that they need the most help with the planning component of self-regulation; without a good plan, we often cannot accomplish our goals (Gaumer Erickson & Noonan, 2021; Gaumer Erickson, Noonan, & Monroe, 2020). Ask your students if they also rated *making plans* as their lowest component.

Explain that we all have strengths and areas for improvement when it comes to self-regulation. Using the information that students wrote down in figure 1.6, have students review the components and specific questionnaire items they noted as strengths and the ones they noted as areas for improvement.

Ask students to share two of their identified questionnaire items with the class—one that they feel is a strength and one that they would like to work on improving. Celebrate the strengths that students share and draw some conclusions for the class as a whole (for example, "It sounds like we, as a group, are good at reflecting. I'm wondering if after practicing self-regulation, our scores in planning may increase."). Emphasize that people, adults included, continue to work on self-regulation throughout their lives.

WHAT TEACHERS SAY

"It was really good for the kids to talk about their struggles amongst themselves and know that they aren't the only ones who may be struggling with not being able to study well, or getting work done, or keeping up with a certain class."

—*Caitlin, technology teacher*

Activity 12: Evaluating Your Efforts

Briefly review the four components of self-regulation (plan, monitor, adjust as needed, and reflect) as outlined in figure 1.2 (page 20). Then, in figure 1.7, have students write down at least three challenging activities, tasks, or goals that they have been working on recently. Instruct students to draw a mark on the arrow for each component to rate how well they used that component in each situation (even if they weren't aware that they were using it at the time). Then have students write a sentence or two about what they did well and how they could improve in the future. The activities can be from school, a job, sports, extracurricular activities, or their personal lives. If students have difficulty identifying activities or goals, encourage them to review their list from activity 3 (page 18).

Activity 13: Journaling for Ongoing Reflection

Summarize that people need to be able to self-regulate to accomplish steps in achieving their goals. Explain that students who have learned about self-regulation (and consistently used it in school) have experienced benefits such as completing more of their homework on time, doing better in their classes, feeling more in control of their learning and their upcoming tasks, getting better organized, managing their time effectively, learning more in their classes, figuring out specific reasons that they are struggling with something and directly addressing those challenges, and gaining a better understanding of how specific actions they take (or don't take) have an impact on their progress and overall success (Gaumer Erickson & Noonan, 2019b). In addition to school-related behaviors, self-regulation can be applied to maintaining control over your emotional reactions or improving musical, artistic, or athletic ability.

Activity or Goal	Plan	Monitor	Adjust	Reflect	What did I do well?	What can I improve?
Example: Eating healthy snacks instead of junk food	Low ←→ High	Low ←→ High	Low ←→ High	Low ←→ High	I planned out the healthy snacks that I would eat and made sure they were available.	I monitored for a couple days, but then I stopped. I ate junk food two days in a row but didn't adjust my plan. I should keep monitoring and adjusting.
	Low ←→ High	Low ←→ High	Low ←→ High	Low ←→ High		
	Low ←→ High	Low ←→ High	Low ←→ High	Low ←→ High		
	Low ←→ High	Low ←→ High	Low ←→ High	Low ←→ High		

FIGURE 1.7: EVALUATING MY EFFORTS.

Visit go.SolutionTree.com/SEL for a free reproducible version of this figure.

Challenge students to write down one thing that they will do over the next few days to improve their self-regulation, focusing on their lowest-scored component from activity 10 (page 25) or activity 12 (page 28). They can choose one of the actions they brainstormed in activity 3 (page 18) or come up with something new that they want to try. Have students journal each day for a week on their effectiveness in their desired behavior (such as strategies they've tried, challenges and successes they have encountered, or adjustments they are making). Promote a collaborative, supportive learning community by providing time for students to reflect on and discuss their efforts toward improved self-regulation.

Summary

Through these facilitated activities, students increase their grasp of the components of self-regulation and understanding of why self-regulation is important now and in the future. They also learn self-appraisal by reflecting on their behaviors, assessing their knowledge, and determining their strengths and areas of need when it comes to self-regulation. The reproducible instructional planning tool provides a guide for planning your instruction. We encourage you to plan instruction and reflect on its effectiveness with colleagues. As students identify their individual strengths and challenges related to self-regulation, they increase their self-awareness and begin to take more responsibility for their actions.

Determine whether you will customize the vignettes or adapt activities to resonate with your students. Then consider how you could provide ongoing practice and feedback to students. Select instructional activities that will help your students meet the initial instruction, guided collaborative learning, and independent practice learning targets.

Understanding Self-Regulation

INSTRUCTIONAL PLANNING TOOL

Initial Instruction: Students describe self-regulation and identify why it is important in their own lives.	
Instructional Activities	Notes and Adaptations
Activity 1: Defining Self-Regulation	
Activity 2: Connecting Intrapersonal Competencies	
Activity 3: We Already Self-Regulate	
Activity 4: Self-Regulation Components	
Activity 5: Check for Understanding	

Guided Collaborative Learning: Students articulate the components of self-regulation and describe the complexity of the self-regulation process.	
Instructional Activities	Notes and Adaptations
Activity 6: Is This Self-Regulation?	
Activity 7: Connecting Outcomes and Behaviors	
Activity 8: Ten Steps to Homework Completion	
Activity 9: Situational Judgment Assessment	

Independent Practice With Feedback: Students reflect on their personal strengths and areas for growth related to the self-regulation components.	
Instructional Activities	Notes and Adaptations
Activity 10: Assessing Your Self-Regulation	
Activity 11: Reflecting on Strengths and Challenges	
Activity 12: Evaluating Your Efforts	
Activity 13: Journaling for Ongoing Reflection	

How will you provide ongoing practice addressing each learning target?

When and how can you provide feedback to each student?

Teaching Self-Regulation © 2022 Solution Tree Press • SolutionTree.com

Visit **go.SolutionTree.com/SEL** to download this free reproducible.

MAKING A PLAN

Planning is the linchpin of self-regulation. As adults, we plan our processes for reaching academic aspirations, enacting healthy behaviors, pursuing career endeavors, and managing emotional reactions—any short- or long-term goal. This goal-directed planning promotes motivation and initiative by helping us focus on cognitive, metacognitive, and physiological factors that influence our success (Usher & Schunk, 2018). Hattie's 2009 synthesis of meta-analyses finds that metacognitive strategies have a high effect size of 0.69 on student achievement, clarifying that "meta-cognitive activities can include planning how to approach a given learning task, evaluating progress, and monitoring comprehension" (p. 188). Along the same lines, in a meta-analysis including thirty-eight studies, Santangelo and colleagues (2016) find that teaching students strategies for planning substantially enhanced the quality of their writing (effect size of 1.06). Planning is a strategy for driving our own success.

WHAT TEACHERS SAY

"I see confidence as a benefit. Students who didn't believe they could create an outline and present an effective three-minute speech did so without much struggle. After the speeches were given, I asked the students if they believed in their ability to complete the speech process. Every student agreed that it was easy. I said, 'Because of your plans and effort to follow them!'"

—Deb, English language arts teacher

Think about a project that your students complete. It might include writing a paper, giving a speech, conducting an experiment, improving the community, or teaching a concept to peers. Planning is necessary for successful project completion, but students need guided practice with feedback to become proficient. We, as caring adults, often regulate for our students by breaking projects down into smaller steps, determining a timeline with short-term due dates, and managing the resources necessary for completion. While these actions of regulating for our students may support their short-term success, we are not fostering *self*-regulation or supporting their long-term success. To shift responsibility to students, we must start by creating an environment for students to practice self-regulation, provide the coaching necessary for success, and offer constructive feedback that supports students in identifying strengths and areas for continued growth.

Now let's return to Mrs. Cooper's class and their research project that we introduced in the previous chapter.

Mrs. Cooper's Research Project

Mrs. Cooper's students have reviewed the research project rubric; reflected on their past research efforts, identifying strengths and areas that were challenging; and set moderately challenging goals that meet mastery criteria. Next, Mrs. Cooper asks the students to brainstorm what it will take to write their best-ever research paper. They work in small groups and then as a whole class to share their ideas while Mrs. Cooper documents all the ideas on the board. The students then categorize the ideas to determine key steps for project completion. In the end, these steps look very similar to the ones that Mrs. Cooper had provided to her students in the past, but she is now seeing students discuss the actions that will be required to complete each step. Students are already more engaged in the research process than they had been in the past.

Now that the steps are identified, Mrs. Cooper asks the class to work together to determine deadlines for completing each step, working backward from the due date. She considers having each student determine individual timelines with progress due dates, but she is nervous about managing so many short-term due dates for this project. To ensure that students still take ownership, she decides to have the class agree on the timeline by expressing their opinions, negotiating, and coming to consensus.

Finally, Mrs. Cooper explains that the timeline is important, but it doesn't provide a true self-regulation plan for *how* the research paper will be completed. To do this, each student will need to write a self-regulation plan that includes when and where they will complete work, the resources they will need, how they will avoid or manage distractions, and other commitments such as sports that may limit time to work on the project. Mrs. Cooper is amazed at the discussions among students about blocking out time to work on the project, using their phones to set reminders, choosing locations that work well for concentration, and strategies such as silencing their phones so that they stay focused. In the end, each student writes a plan for completing the research and writing the paper.

Mrs. Cooper reviews each plan and provides feedback by prompting each student to expand his or her plan based on her prior knowledge of the student. She sighs in relief—the research project is underway, and she feels confident that all students understand the expectations and the process for completing the research paper.

WHAT STUDENTS SAY

"I'm terrible at planning. I just wait for the teacher to tell me what to do."

—Tenth-grade student

Self-regulation has implications for all aspects of our lives. Elite athletes plan their workouts to ensure their best performance, performers dedicate substantial time to practice, and employees complete tasks in a timely manner. We self-regulate everything from our emotional reactions to personal and professional goals that require years of sustained effort to achieve. However, students report that they do not know how to effectively plan for success and often rely on others to direct their actions. When students are asked about behaviors associated with self-regulation, their lowest self-identified area is *planning*. Results from 18,154 students from the United States on the self-report section of the Self-Regulation Questionnaire and Knowledge Test demonstrate that 52 percent of students rated themselves the lowest in the planning component of self-regulation, compared to 20 percent for monitoring, 19 percent for adjusting, and 9 percent for reflecting (Gaumer Erickson et al., 2020). The instructional activities in this chapter are designed to increase students' understanding of the *planning* component of self-regulation and promote the development of detailed, proactive self-regulation plans across a variety of contexts. The activities are ordered from highly structured to authentic independent practice with feedback.

Outline of Instructional Activities

- **Initial Instruction:** Your goal is for students to be able to differentiate between a goal and a plan and describe a variety of areas in life in which self-regulation planning is beneficial.

  - ➤ **Activity 14**—Why Do We Plan?

  - ➤ **Activity 15**—Planning Emotional Regulation

  - ➤ **Activity 16**—Reflecting on My Academic Planning

  - ➤ **Activity 17**—Common Planning Elements

  - ➤ **Activity 18**—Check for Understanding

- **Guided Collaborative Learning:** Your goal is for students to be able to determine behaviors, processes, and timelines for situation-specific, quality self-regulation planning.

  ➤ **Activity 19**—Ava Wants More Energy—Planning for Healthy Eating

  ➤ **Activity 20**—Anthony Wants to Save Money—Budgeting

  ➤ **Activity 21**—Olivia Needs a Homework Plan—Planning for Academic Success

  ➤ **Activity 22**—Levi's Anxiety Over Public Speaking—Strategies for Physiological Reactions

  ➤ **Activity 23**—Situational Judgment Assessment

- **Independent Practice With Feedback:** Your goal is for students to identify specific outcomes that they want to accomplish and create personalized, detailed self-regulation plans for reaching their goals.

  ➤ **Activity 24**—Developing Your Self-Regulation Plan

  ➤ **Activity 25**—Planning for Success on an Assignment or Project

Initial Instruction

Through these activities, students learn critical concepts, make connections to their lives, and build a shared vocabulary. Your goal is for students to be able to differentiate between a goal and a plan and describe a variety of areas in life in which self-regulation planning is beneficial.

Activity 14: Why Do We Plan?

Display the quote, "A goal without a plan is just a wish" (Antoine de Saint-Exupéry; Goodreads, n.d.a). In small groups or as a whole class, discuss the following prompts.

- What does this quote mean?

- How does this apply to us?

- Have you had goals that you didn't reach because you didn't plan?

Using a Venn diagram, have students compare and contrast the terms *goal* and *plan*. Students can refer to figure 1.5 (page 23) that they completed in activity 7 for examples of goals with associated self-regulation behaviors. Emphasize that both goals and plans help us focus and guide our behavior, whether it be for academics, health, or social interactions. Planning is how we enact goal-directed behaviors over time. A goal tells us where we are going; a plan tells us how we will get there.

"Students said, 'Okay. I can do this. I do have goals. They may not be the same as my partner or the girl sitting next to me, but they're mine and they're specific to me and catered to me, and I have the resources to accomplish them.'"

—Hanna, English language arts teacher

Activity 15: Planning Emotional Regulation

Introduce students to the concept of regulating emotional reactions by showing a short video, such as this one from the Sentis (2012) Brain Animation Series: "Emotions and the Brain" (https://youtube.com/watch?v=x NY0AAUtH3g). After watching the video, explain to students that we all feel a range of emotions throughout a day—this is healthy and natural. However, it is important to regulate how we *express* those emotions. We have more control over emotional reactions when we use coping mechanisms or calming strategies.

Display the feeling words wheel, shown in figure 2.1 (page 38), to assist students in identifying emotions. Have students work with a partner to review and discuss some of the complex feelings from the two outer rings. Emphasize the fact that feelings often cause physiological changes to our bodies, and prompt students to discuss physical changes (such as increased heart rate, feeling hot, and turning red) they have experienced with the complex feelings.

In small groups, have students discuss coping mechanisms, strategies, or tools they have used or could use to manage their emotional reactions. These might include taking deep breaths, going for a walk, counting to ten before responding, finding a quiet place, or doing yoga. Encourage each group to share three ideas with the class. Write down responses as students share them. Consider displaying the responses on an anchor chart in the classroom so students can refer to the list when needed. Debrief by explaining to students that without a plan, we often are at a loss for how to cope with intense emotions. If we plan specific strategies, such as counting to ten, we can start to manage our emotional reactions. Not all strategies work for everyone, so it is important to try out different ones to determine when and how to use them.

"We use the feelings word wheel frequently in literature [class] to express our feelings and how to communicate."

—Sandy, middle school teacher

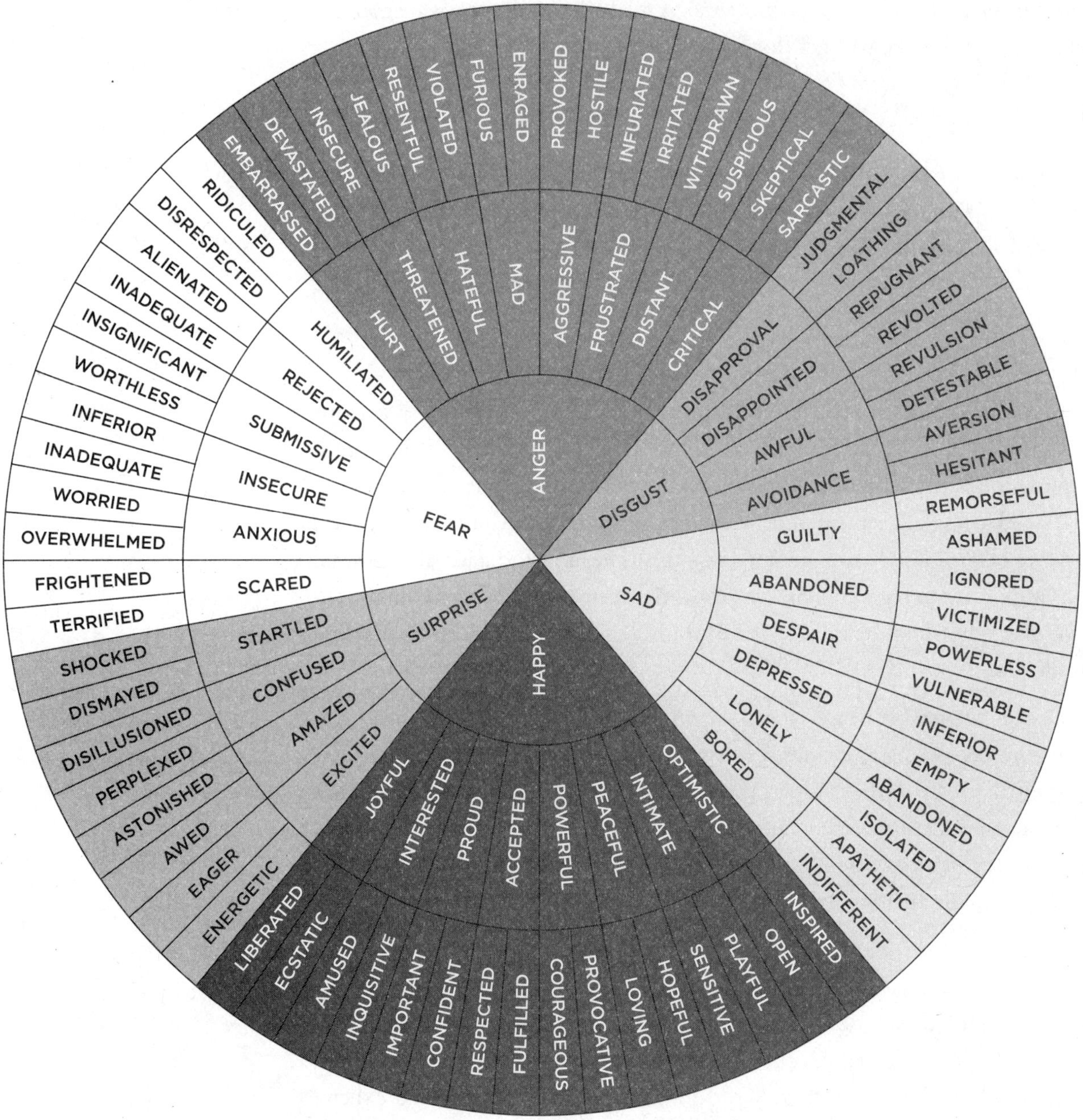

Source: Adapted with permission from the publisher, Thinkmap, Inc. Copyright ©1998–2018. All rights reserved. For more information, visit https://www.vocabulary.com.

FIGURE 2.1: FEELING WORDS WHEEL.

Visit ***go.SolutionTree.com/SEL*** *for a free reproducible version of this figure.*

Activity 16: Reflecting on My Academic Planning

Ask students to spend a few minutes individually completing figure 2.2 by reflecting on how they currently approach challenging assignments, projects, or tests. Encourage students to share their ratings and justifications in small groups or with partners, looking for similarities. Debrief by explaining that most people start out with vague plans, but together we are going to learn the value of detailed preparation. Planning reduces anxiety and frees up time for us to not only get our work done but to incorporate fun activities into our schedules. Review the students' answers, comparing to your perceptions of the student and determining commonalities throughout the class in planning. (We will return to this figure in activity 25: Planning for Success on an Assignment or Project, page 51.)

Planning is important for academic success. How do you approach difficult assignments, projects, or preparing for tests?			
Approaches	**Questions to Think About**	**Rate Yourself (10 = Strong; 1 = Weak)**	**Write a sentence justifying your rating.**
Self-directing	Do you make your own plan? OR Do you wait for someone else (teacher, parent, friend, and so on) to tell you how to proceed?		
Detailing actions	Does your plan include lots of details? OR Is your plan more of a broad outline? Do you dive straight in and immediately start working without planning?		
Managing time	Do you think about how long each step will take you and block out work or study time? OR Do you just figure it out as you go?		
Focusing attention	Do you think about what might get in the way of completing your plan? Do you plan out ways you will avoid distractions? OR Do you consider the distractions as they occur?		
Ongoing tracking	Do you identify ways to track your progress? OR Do you wait until you're prompted to track your progress?		
Reflecting on past efforts	Do you consider how you've completed prior difficult tasks? OR Do you treat each situation as new, without thinking too much about the past?		

FIGURE 2.2: REFLECTING ON ACADEMIC PLANNING.

*Visit **go.SolutionTree.com/SEL** for a free reproducible version of this figure.*

Activity 17: Common Planning Elements

At this point, students may have a strong sense that planning is important, so it is time to think about how to plan effectively. As a class, discuss with and prompt students to identify how they could apply six common elements of self-regulation plans, outlined in figure 2.3, to a commonplace personal goal, such as getting stronger or more fit. For example, if your goal is to get stronger, you could take the following six steps.

1. Make a to-do list of the exercises that you'll do daily.

2. Schedule a specific time each day to work out, setting reminders on your phone.

3. Determine dates that you'll reflect on your fitness progress.

4. Outline strategies, such as doing your favorite exercise first if you're feeling tired, or repeating a positive mantra such as "practice makes progress" or "all progress is good progress" if you are frustrated that you aren't seeing your strength increasing as quickly as you had hoped.

5. Put your phone in airplane mode if social media is distracting but you still want to listen to music you have downloaded.

6. Find a friend to work out with you, providing encouragement and pushing you to give maximum effort.

Your students will likely contribute numerous additional examples. Wrap up the discussion by noting that the more elements included in a plan, the greater your likelihood of success.

Activity 18: Check for Understanding

Using response cards or an online quiz platform, gather individual students' responses to the items displayed in figure 2.4. Review the responses to ensure that students understand the concept of planning. Reteach as necessary. [The answer key for figure 2.4 is: 1–true; 2–true; 3–false; 4–c.]

Guided Collaborative Learning

Scenario-based activities address an array of circumstances to which adolescents can relate. Through these collaborative-learning activities, students articulate behaviors for situation-specific, quality self-regulation planning. Your goal is for students to be able to determine behaviors, processes, and timelines for situation-specific, quality self-regulation planning.

My goal or outcome: _____		
Planning element	**Description**	**What could this look like for the goal?**
To-do list	Listing specific actions or tasks that need to be completed	
Schedule	Identifying a specific time to focus on the ongoing tasks; setting reminders	
Timeline	Outlining when each step needs to be completed to meet a deadline; determining when you will monitor progress toward your goal	
Emotional triggers and response options	Thinking about potential feelings you might encounter while working on your plan, and then identifying how you will address your emotional reactions so that you can keep making progress	
Managing distractions	Identifying potential distractions and determining how you will eliminate or manage them	
Accountability partner	Asking a friend to check in with you or participate in your activities or tasks; providing support, encouragement, and honest constructive feedback to each other	

FIGURE 2.3: COMMON ELEMENTS OF SELF-REGULATION PLANS.

Visit go.SolutionTree.com/SEL for a free reproducible version of this figure.

Planning Elements

True or False

1. _____ If you plan, you are more likely to resist distractions and manage your actions.

2. _____ If you plan, you are better able to manage your reactions when you are feeling stressed.

3. _____ A goal and a plan are actually the same thing.

Multiple Choice

4. Identify the best option to address the problem of being late to school.

    a. Telling your mom about the problem and asking her to get you to school on time

    b. Setting an extra alarm tomorrow to make it more likely that you will get up on time

    c. Considering possible reasons for your tardiness (such as staying up too late or not gathering supplies until morning) and making a plan to address those things

    d. Deciding that now that you're aware of the issue, you won't have trouble tomorrow—you know you just need to get up with your alarm

FIGURE 2.4: CHECK FOR UNDERSTANDING—PLANNING ELEMENTS.

Visit go.SolutionTree.com/SEL for a free reproducible version of this figure.

Activity 19: Ava Wants More Energy—Planning for Healthy Eating

Read the scenario as a class and discuss Ava's plan for eating healthier. This scenario is reproducible from appendix C (page 163). We will return to this scenario in activity 58 (page 104) and in activity 69 (page 118).

SCENARIO

Ava lacks energy and spends too much money on energy drinks and cookies (her daily lunch). She falls asleep every afternoon in algebra and doesn't feel well in general. She wants to eat healthier. She decides to change her diet to low-sugar, minimally processed food, and shift to eating more protein, fruits, and vegetables. She gives away all her energy drinks and writes out a menu of what she will eat for breakfast, lunch, dinner, and snacks (using a nutritional guidance website to make sure that her menus will help her meet her goals). She discusses the plan with her family and asks her mom to stop buying cookies. She then records her food intake using an app. She gets off track at a weekend party, eating chips and cookies. The next day, she decides to keep granola bars and dried fruit in her purse so that she has an alternative to chips and cookies when at parties. Each day she reviews the data in the app, tracking nutrients consumed in relation to recommended daily allowances, and thinks about whether she ate a balanced diet that followed her menu. Using a printed calendar, Ava gives herself one to five stars for her effort that day and writes one personal success or challenge she experienced. Weekly, she thinks about what is working and what isn't, and then she revises her plan accordingly. She now has much more energy, stays awake in algebra, and feels healthier overall.

You can guide the discussion by displaying and prompting students to consider how Ava addressed the four components of self-regulation—plan, monitor, adjust, and reflect—as shown in figure 1.2 (page 20).

1. What was included in Ava's plan?

2. How did she monitor?

3. How did she adjust her plan? Did she ask others for help?

4. How did she reflect? Was Ava more successful because she followed the self-regulation process?

Emphasize that Ava designed a detailed *plan* that includes multiple actions (making a menu, getting rid of unhealthy food, tracking her food intake). After the obstacle of unhealthy food at a party, Ava *adjusted* her plan by keeping healthy snacks in her purse. She *monitored* and reflected daily by reviewing the data on the app, giving herself stars for effort, and writing out personal successes and challenges. She also *reflected* weekly by thinking through the effectiveness of her plan and identifying adjustments she could make for the following week.

Activity 20: Anthony Wants to Save Money—Budgeting

Provide students with an example (you can use the following one or create your own) in which a youth is trying to save money for a large purchase (see also activity 34 [page 65] and activity 46 [page 85] for the continuation of this scenario). This scenario is reproducible from appendix C (page 163). Working in small groups, ask students to make a plan for how the person will reach the goal.

SCENARIO

Anthony wants to save money for a gaming system. He has a part-time job and makes about $80 per week. Anthony usually spends all his money going out to eat with friends. Anthony knows that he's going to need to use self-regulation to save the money for the gaming system.

As groups discuss, use the following prompts to deepen their thinking.

- What steps could Anthony take to save his money? Note, steps need to be actions instead of just not doing something. If he is *not* spending his money on food, what will he *do* to see friends and eat socially? This should all be part of the plan.

- What could go wrong, and what could Anthony do to prevent this from derailing his plan?

- Realistically, how long will it take Anthony to save enough for a gaming system?

Ask each group to briefly present their plan for Anthony. As the groups share, note similarities and differences among the plans. Emphasize that our plans don't look exactly the same—we are all unique and so are the plans we develop. Wrap up the discussion by asking students for a show of hands to answer questions such as, "How many of you are trying or would like to save money? Do you have a plan for saving money? Is it as detailed as Anthony's plan?" Ask students if they think that detailed planning is more likely to lead to the desired goal than vague planning.

Activity 21: Olivia Needs a Homework Plan— Planning for Academic Success

Tell students that, although we might think our task is simple (and therefore only needs a simple plan for accomplishing it), things are almost always more complicated than we originally think. With certain tasks that we do often, like completing our homework, we might complete a lot of the steps automatically without thinking about them, or even realizing that we've done them. When we succeed at accomplishing the task, that's not necessarily a problem. But if we're having trouble accomplishing the task successfully, it's important to think about the small details that we usually overlook, because that might be where the problem is occurring. To illustrate this point, read the following scenario and then have students work in small groups to create a detailed plan for homework completion. This scenario is referenced again in activity 35 (page 66) and is reproducible from appendix C (page 163).

SCENARIO

Your younger sister, Olivia, who is in sixth grade, has been having trouble finishing her homework. She knows that lately you've been doing a lot better at turning things in on time, so she asks you to help her figure out how she can improve. You've been using self-regulation to increase your success, and you know that, in general, students who use self-regulation are more likely to complete their homework on time. You decide that the best way to support your sister is by helping her brainstorm a self-regulation plan for her homework completion.

After giving students time to read the scenario, have them work in small groups to brainstorm the steps that they would need to include in the plan for homework completion. If they completed activity 8 (page 24) in chapter 1, they can use their ten steps to homework completion to guide their planning for Olivia. A fourteen-step example plan that is similar to what students may develop follows in figure 2.5.

Olivia's Homework Plan Example

1. Write down each assignment in a planner; include when the assignment is due.

2. Review all assignment due dates and prioritize the ones due the next day or in the near future (the next couple of days).

3. Create a list of homework tasks to accomplish today. Make sure to include steps toward big projects.

4. Determine a specific time to start homework (like 4:30 p.m.) and set an alarm for that time as a reminder to start.

5. Near the end of the school day, check the planner to review the list of after-school tasks and include all necessary supplies to take home.

6. At 4:30, start by deciding on the order for completing each task or assignment and estimate how long each task will take to complete. Write the estimated time in the planner.

7. Set an alarm for 5:15 p.m. to check on progress.

8. Work on homework in a room with soft background music to mask other sounds in the house.

9. When the 5:15 alarm goes off to check progress, review the planner and check off all finished assignments; determine whether each assignment required the allotted time, and write down the actual amount of time spent on each assignment. Determine how much more time is needed to finish homework.

10. Think through distractions. If your phone is a distraction, put it on silent mode and only check it during breaks. If a sibling is a distraction, tell him or her that you are working on homework and ask if you can wait until your next scheduled break to talk or play. If music is a distraction, shut it off or switch to instrumentals. If location is a distraction, move to the kitchen table or another location where you will be able to focus.

11. If you need a break, take one. But before you start the break, be sure to set an alarm as a reminder for when to return to homework. When the alarm goes off, finish the remaining homework.

12. Check off all assignments in the planner once finished; write down the time spent on each assignment. Review time estimated for task completion and actual time required, then use this information to estimate the time necessary for future homework tasks.

13. Put all homework and necessary supplies in your backpack, so you don't forget them the next day.

14. Turn in homework at school the next day. Consider progress on longer-term assignments and plan tasks for after school.

FIGURE 2.5: OLIVIA'S HOMEWORK PLAN EXAMPLE.

Visit go.SolutionTree.com/SEL for a free reproducible version of this figure.

To ensure that the homework plan is thorough and addresses all the necessary pieces, students can use targeted questions when helping someone else create a plan (and when creating their own plans). To demonstrate this, ask students to raise their hand if their group's plan addresses the homework prompts outlined in figure 2.6 (page 46). Read each prompt, wait for students to determine if their plan would answer the question, and then call on students to share how their plan addresses the question. If a group's plan did not address the question, have them write down the question so that they can add a step to address it.

Homework Prompts

- What homework do you have?
- What materials do you need to complete the homework?
- How long do you think it will take to finish your homework?
- What else do you have planned for today?
- When will you start working on your homework?
- Where will you work on it?
- What distractions are likely to get in your way? How will you reduce or eliminate these distractions?
- Will you need breaks? When will you take these breaks; how long will they last?
- Will you need help? If yes, how will you get help?
- When will you have the homework finished?
- How will you determine if you are on track to finish the homework by your planned deadline? What will you do if you aren't on track?
- How will you make sure that you turn in your homework to your teacher (instead of forgetting it somewhere)?
- How and when will you reflect on the effectiveness of your plan and determine adjustments?

FIGURE 2.6: HOMEWORK PROMPTS.

*Visit **go.SolutionTree.com/SEL** for a free reproducible version of this figure.*

To wrap up the discussion, emphasize again that things that initially seem simple are usually more complex. Tell students that the most effective self-regulation plans include a lot of details (such as specific actions or steps, how and when you will complete each step, possible complications you might encounter and how you will address them, how you will monitor your progress, and how you will learn from the experience). Especially when you are working on tasks that you do on a regular basis but become challenging, it's important to include details for several reasons: (a) it helps ensure that you are not forgetting an important part of the process because it has become so routine that you don't even think about it, (b) it makes it less likely that you'll get off track because you were surprised by something that you could have planned for, and (c) it helps you identify unexpected areas that are contributing to your current struggles with the task.

Activity 22: Levi's Anxiety Over Public Speaking— Strategies for Physiological Reactions

Emphasize that it is normal to have a wide range of emotions and that often emotions can cause physiological reactions. Remind students that when we experience intense or stressful emotions, we can use coping mechanisms or calming strategies to help regulate those emotions and the physiological reactions they inspire. As a class, read the following scenario and then work to create a detailed plan for regulating emotional reactions in this situation. This scenario is reproducible from appendix C (page 163). An example of a completed plan is provided in activity 36 (page 67).

SCENARIO

Your friend Levi is taking a public speaking class. He knows that he will be expected to speak in front of groups in the career he plans to pursue. The only problem is that Levi gets very anxious when speaking in front of a group. His palms sweat and his mouth gets very dry. He ends up talking too fast and without emotion. Help Levi make a plan for reducing his anxiety and effectively conveying his ideas to a group.

In small groups, ask students to come up with a plan that Levi could use to be more effective when expressing his ideas while speaking in public. Use the guiding questions in figure 2.7 to create a plan. The plan should include Levi's preparation for the speech as well as calming techniques that he can employ before giving the speech.

Guiding Questions for Emotional Regulation

1. What emotions are occurring?
2. What physiological reactions are being experienced?
3. What actions could be taken to prepare for the emotional situation?
4. What actions could be taken to address the emotional reaction?
5. How might the situation be reframed to be less stress inducing?
6. How might reflection inform future situations?

FIGURE 2.7: GUIDING QUESTIONS FOR EMOTIONAL REGULATION.

*Visit **go.SolutionTree.com/SEL** for a free reproducible version of this figure.*

Have groups exchange plans, discuss, and provide feedback to each other. This feedback should include at least two strengths and one question about or suggestion for the plan. Then ask each group to report out one unique or interesting idea from the plan that they reviewed. Use the example plan in activity 36 (page 67) to guide groups if their plans lack detail.

To extend the activity, ask students to think about goals or tasks that have caused them anxiety in the past. Explain that they can write a plan for using self-regulation to deal with that anxiety. In their plan, they should identify how they are feeling and what about the situation or experience causes them to feel that way. They should then identify strategies (refer to the anchor chart created in activity 15, page 37) that they think would help them reduce anxiety.

WHAT STUDENTS SAY

"Before giving my physics presentation, I will use slow diaphragmatic breathing to calm my nerves."

—Twelfth-grade student

Activity 23: Situational Judgment Assessment

Ask students to independently read the following scenario and answer the prompt. This scenario extends through each chapter, building on prior answers. A reproducible form with all situational judgment assessments is provided in appendix A (page 153).

SCENARIO

In health class, Alex and his classmates learned about the benefits of drinking an adequate amount of water each day. Alex has decided that he does not drink enough water.

Make a five-step daily plan for Alex that will result in his increased water consumption. Assume that Alex goes to your school and participates in the same classes and extracurricular activities as you.

Review each student's answers to determine whether the steps identified would likely increase Alex's water intake. Were five distinct steps identified? Which common planning elements (see figure 2.3, page 41) are included? Do the steps address obstacles such as not having water with you? Is a monitoring method included in the plan? Provide specific, constructive feedback to each student.

Independent Practice With Feedback

Through independent practice, students begin applying their learning to their own endeavors. This promotes fluency of the skills and provides opportunities for formative feedback and coaching. Your goal is for students to identify specific outcomes they want to accomplish and create personalized, detailed self-regulation plans for reaching their goals.

"When [my teacher] started talking to us about self-regulation, I noticed that I have no self-regulation whatsoever. I never respect deadlines, and I always rush to get my work done at the very last minute. Self-regulation did really help me complete the assignment on time and do it well. I did actually make a plan before doing this, which helped me to get it done faster . . . . I decided to write a great newsletter."

—Tenth-grade student

Activity 24: Developing Your Self-Regulation Plan

Explain to students that they are going to make a plan to accomplish a short-term goal of their own. Have students choose something that is important to them (such as passing the driver's license exam, getting to school or work on time, writing better essays, increasing fitness, or handling stress), within their control (for example, *applying* for jobs rather than *getting* a job), and that can be enacted over the next few weeks. If students are struggling to choose a goal, have them refer to the list they created in activity 3 (page 18) of things that they wanted to get better at self-regulating.

Tell students that they will put their plans into practice over the next few weeks, and in future class sessions, they will work on how to monitor their plans, adjust when things aren't working, and reflect on their efforts and progress toward accomplishing their goals. Just like the plans that they wrote for Anthony to save money, for Olivia who wanted help getting homework done on time, and for Levi to reduce anxiety during public speaking, they should create detailed plans that include a realistic timeline, the steps that they will need to do along the way, and a list of potential barriers and obstacles they might encounter (along with the strategies they will use to overcome those barriers and obstacles).

Remind students that good plans will address all of the following questions in detail.

- How will I know I've successfully reached my goal? What does success look like?

- What are the steps, strategies, and actions necessary to accomplish my goal? When, where, and how will I work toward my goal?

- What could go wrong? How will I avoid or overcome these challenges?

- How will I track my progress?

Have students record their goal; the steps, strategies, or actions they need to take to accomplish it (their plan); and possible challenges that might arise with ways to address those challenges and keep moving forward. Remind them to be as detailed as possible.

My goal:

My plan:

Possible challenges and ways to address them:

Have students share their plans with a partner and discuss. Ask partners to provide suggestions for improving the plan. When giving each other feedback, students can reflect on the prompts outlined in figure 2.8.

Feedback Prompts for Planning

1. Does the plan include all or most of the common planning elements? If not, which ones could be added to improve the plan?

   - To-do list: Listing specific actions or tasks that need to be completed

   - Schedule: Identifying a specific time to focus on the ongoing tasks; setting reminders

   - Timeline: Outlining when each step needs to be completed in order to meet an overall deadline; determining when you will monitor progress toward your goal

   - Emotional triggers and response options: Thinking about potential feelings you might encounter while working on your plan, and then identifying how you will address your emotional reactions so that you can keep making progress

   - Managing distractions: Identifying potential distractions and determining how you will eliminate or manage them

   - Accountability partner: Asking a friend to check in with you or participate in your activities or tasks; providing support, encouragement, and honest constructive feedback to each other

2. What might get in the way of completing the plan? What could be changed or added to the plan to prevent it from going off track?

3. Can the plan be completed independently or will help be required (such as transportation to a job interview or help opening a savings account)? If help is needed, what are the steps to getting that help?

4. How confident am I that the steps in the plan include everything necessary to ensure success? If I'm not confident, how would I suggest further improving the plan?

FIGURE 2.8: FEEDBACK PROMPTS FOR PLANNING.

*Visit **go.SolutionTree.com/SEL** for a free reproducible version of this figure.*

Have each student finalize and submit a completed plan. Provide feedback on each plan, noting at least two positive aspects and one thing that the student might want to consider to improve his or her plan. You can incorporate these plans, or the plans from activity 25, into application activities in chapters 3–5 for the other components of self-regulation: monitor, adjust, and reflect.

Activity 25: Planning for Success on an Assignment or Project

Prompt each student to create a personal plan for an upcoming project, to prepare for a test, or complete daily assignments. Students can refer to their individual reflection on academic planning outlined in figure 2.2 (page 39), thinking about their past behaviors in order to design plans that meet their needs. As a class, discuss the following steps, brainstorm options with students, and note ideas that they want to incorporate into their plans.

Step One: Visualize Success

Even if the goal seems as simple as turning in homework on time, have students visualize and discuss success. What are the advantages of turning homework in on time? What does quality homework look like (for example, completing the entire assignment, double checking answers, asking a friend if I'm not sure of a concept, and so on)? Prompt students to document their visualized success in the form of a goal or an outcome. An example template is provided in appendix D (page 171).

Step Two: Set Up Your Workspace

Explain to students that identifying a workspace and setting it up according to your specific needs for studying and working on homework can help you stay focused on your work. Even though students may not have control over all aspects of their workspace (such as a kitchen table at home rather than a desk), they can control aspects such as having all needed materials together and reducing distractions by techniques such as wearing headphones and muting social media notifications on their phones.

Discuss the following questions, prompting students to note ideas they will incorporate into their plans.

- What are some possible places in your house that could become a workspace for you? The kitchen or dining room table? Your bed? A favorite chair in your living room?

> ➤ Which space do you think will help you be comfortable but still able to focus on your work?

>> ➤ What supplies do you think you might need to have in your workspace or close by? For instance, do you need a computer? Paper and pen? Textbooks? Water? Other supplies and resources?

- What distractions are likely to get in your way?

- How will you reduce or eliminate these distractions?

- What time of day will you complete work?

- Will you need breaks? When will you take these breaks? How long will they last?

Step Three: Prioritize Your Work

Whether completing a project or organizing daily assignments, it is helpful to determine an order in which you will complete the tasks. For a project, this likely looks like a timeline with self-imposed, short-term due dates. For daily homework, this becomes more of an everyday process of determining homework and then prioritizing it based on factors such as difficulty or likelihood of needing to ask for help. As students discuss ideas for prioritizing their work, use the following prompts when needed.

- What homework do you have? Are there some long-term assignments and some short-term assignments? Are some assignments higher priorities than others?

- How long do you think it will take to finish the work?

- What else do you have planned—for the day, the week, and so on?

- When will you start working on your homework?

- Will you need help? If yes, how will you get this help?

- When will you have the homework done?

- How will you determine if you are on track to get the homework done according to your plan? What will you do if you aren't on track?

- How will you make sure that you get your completed homework turned in to your teacher?

Step Four: Write Your Plan

After brainstorming options, prompt students to write their own self-regulation plans. An example template is provided in appendix D (page 171). While this template will guide students' planning, as they get more proficient at self-regulation, encourage students to design their own templates or processes for planning.

Using the prompts outlined in figure 2.8 (page 50), pair students to provide each other feedback that leads to expansion of their plans. Each plan should be unique to the student, promoting his or her success.

Provide feedback on each plan, noting at least two positive aspects and one thing that the student might want to consider to improve his or her plan. You can incorporate these plans, or the plans from activity 24, into application activities in chapters 3–5 for the other components of self-regulation: monitor, adjust, and reflect.

WHAT TEACHERS SAY

"On Monday, each student made a plan for the week. On Tuesday, students reviewed their plans, checked progress, and checked any grades that had gotten posted. On Wednesday, students reviewed their plans again, asking, 'Is it working? Where am I at?' Thursday they kind of reevaluated if there was anything they needed to change or do differently for Thursday and Friday. And then Friday they just reflected about the whole week, asking, 'What went well? What didn't go well? What is my progress?' One of the things that I was not really anticipating and expecting, but was delighted to see, was that students started to really change their behavior in class. I had other teachers coming to me and saying, 'Man, I don't know what you're doing with these kids, but they're paying attention and it's different.' Not only is their behavior improving, but their academics are also improving, they're taking ownership and responsibility for their grades, and I'm super excited for them to do that at this age because that will only help them in the future."

—Heidi, sixth-grade teacher

Summary

Through these facilitated activities, students learn the importance of detailed planning and practice designing self-regulation plans for a variety of outcomes. The reproducible instructional planning tool (page 54) provides a guide for planning your instruction. Students will continue to build plans for personal or academic endeavors in the following chapters by learning to monitor, adjust, and reflect on their efforts. Facilitated planning leads to enhanced student ownership over their own success, thereby increasing motivation and engagement.

Determine whether you will customize the vignettes or adapt activities to resonate with your students. Then consider how you could provide ongoing practice and feedback to students. Select instructional activities that will help your students meet the initial instruction, guided collaborative learning, and independent practice learning targets.

Making a Plan

INSTRUCTIONAL PLANNING TOOL

Initial Instruction: Students differentiate between a goal and a plan and describe a variety of areas in life in which self-regulation planning is beneficial.

Instructional Activities	Notes and Adaptations
Activity 14: Why Do We Plan?	
Activity 15: Planning Emotional Regulation	
Activity 16: Reflecting on My Academic Planning	
Activity 17: Common Planning Elements	
Activity 18: Check for Understanding	

Guided Collaborative Learning: Students determine behaviors, processes, and timelines for situation-specific quality self-regulation planning.

Instructional Activities	Notes and Adaptations
Activity 19: Ava Wants More Energy—Planning for Healthy Eating	
Activity 20: Anthony Wants to Save Money—Budgeting	
Activity 21: Olivia Needs a Homework Plan—Planning for Academic Success	
Activity 22: Levi's Anxiety Over Public Speaking—Strategies for Physiological Reactions	
Activity 23: Situational Judgment Assessment	

Independent Practice With Feedback: Students identify specific outcomes that they want to accomplish and create personalized, detailed, self-regulation plans for reaching their goals.

Instructional Activities	Notes and Adaptations
Activity 24: Developing Your Self-Regulation Plan	
Activity 25: Planning for Success on an Assignment or Project	

How will you provide ongoing practice addressing each learning target?

When and how can you provide feedback to each student?

Teaching Self-Regulation © 2022 Solution Tree Press • SolutionTree.com

Visit **go.SolutionTree.com/SEL** to download this free reproducible.

MONITORING YOUR PLAN AND PROGRESS

A key component of self-regulation is monitoring, which requires students to continually pay attention to how they are progressing toward their objectives. To effectively self-regulate after we create a plan, we must monitor both our actions (whether we are carrying out the plan as intended) and our progress toward meeting the objective. In this way, we continually self-assess our performance and increase our self-awareness, or understanding of our own strengths, areas for growth, preferences, and interests. For example, if you designed a fitness plan to grow stronger, you would monitor your actions (such as the exercises that you are doing to build strength) and your progress (whether you are getting stronger). Self-monitoring has been researched extensively across fields. In a meta-analysis, self-monitoring was found to have a large positive effect on reading performance for students in elementary and secondary schools (Guzman, Goldberg, & Swanson, 2018). In a sample of college students, self-monitoring was positively associated with critical thinking (Ghanizadeh, 2017). In medicine, it has been shown to be an essential element of chronic disease management (Jiang & Cameron, 2020). Monitoring is a self-appraisal skill that builds self-awareness and promotes continued focus on behaviors that lead to successful outcomes.

WHAT STUDENTS SAY

"I used to think that monitoring was just checking things off a list, but now I understand that it is so much more."

—Seventh-grade student

Think about your students. What do the successful students do? Actions likely include taking notes in class, using designated class time to start homework, asking questions if confused, completing and turning in homework on time, preparing prior to and actively participating during class, and working collaboratively with other students. Adept learners continually monitor their successful behaviors in addition to their progress in mastering concepts. Monitoring increases self-awareness, which helps us plan and adjust our behaviors whenever needed.

Now let's return to Mrs. Cooper's freshmen language arts class.

Mrs. Cooper's Research Project

Students are busy working on their research papers, and the first short-term deadline has arrived. Mrs. Cooper knows that this is a key moment to support students' monitoring of both their progress and the specific actions that contribute to that progress.

Mrs. Cooper considers making a worksheet with questions like the following.

- Did I meet today's deadline?

- Is my work of high quality?

- Is my self-regulation plan working effectively?

- Are there changes that I need to make to stay on track with the research and writing?

But instead of making this monitoring form, she decides that if she wants students to self-monitor, they will benefit from determining their own prompts to guide their monitoring efforts. She asks the class, "What do we need to monitor?" They quickly respond that they need to monitor whether they got the first task turned in on time. Mrs. Cooper agrees and writes this on the board. She then asks, "What else?" It requires some wait time, but students begin to respond with ideas that Mrs. Cooper adds to the board. Mrs. Cooper reminds students that they not only need to monitor progress toward their goal, but they also need to monitor the actions that are helping them succeed. With shoulder partners, students work to come up with actions that they could monitor. They then share ideas as a class. Now Mrs. Cooper has a long list on the board that includes actions to monitor regarding when and where work was completed; how much time was devoted to the project; and challenges such as finding research articles, having adequately detailed source notes, and ensuring the outline is specific enough.

She then asks students, "If this is what we need to monitor, how are we going to do so?" Some students say that Mrs. Cooper should give them a form to fill out on each due date. Mrs. Cooper smiles, as this was her original plan. But then other students add ideas like keeping a checklist with them that they can use every day to make sure they are following the actions listed on their plan (for instance, working on the project for an hour each day) or making a virtual form to track their progress. Another group of students talks about using their planners that were given out at the beginning of the school year and writing about their progress on each date in the planner, or using the calendars on their phones to monitor by creating entries for each due date and adding event details to take notes about what's working or needs to be adjusted.

Mrs. Cooper is now a little nervous. The students came up with a lot of great ideas. Does she make them pick one so that it's easier for her to track? She thinks about how she monitors her own actions like getting homework graded, drinking enough water daily, or getting to bed at a reasonable hour. She realizes that she uses numerous methods for monitoring and wouldn't want to be limited by a teacher's requirement. Mrs. Cooper decides that students can choose their method but that they must collaborate with other students who choose the same method to determine what they will monitor, when they will monitor, and how they will document the monitoring. Thirty minutes later, each group is ready to share their monitoring plan with the whole class.

Mrs. Cooper makes a note of the monitoring technique each student selected and decides that, on the short-term due dates, she will provide class time for the groups to work together to analyze each other's monitoring efforts. Mrs. Cooper also plans to use independent work time for individual student conferences by calling students up to her desk to discuss their progress. Mrs. Cooper reflects on the fact that students came up with more detailed monitoring techniques than she would have required. So far students are engaged and on track.

Numerous monitoring techniques (such as checklists, logs, learning journals, rubrics, and progress graphs) demonstrate effectiveness (Ramdass & Zimmerman, 2011; Zimmerman & Kitsantas, 2014). While the strategies may vary based on personal preferences and the task, frequent monitoring helps students stay on track and deepen their learning. These techniques also help students identify misunderstandings or gaps between their efforts and the desired outcomes (Frey et al., 2018). The instructional activities in this chapter are designed to increase students' abilities to monitor both progress and actions, as well as determine effective monitoring strategies based on their personal preferences and the desired outcome. By the independent practice stage, students will incorporate personalized methods for monitoring progress and actions within their self-regulation plans.

WHAT TEACHERS SAY

"They did the work of mapping out the calendar days and setting some benchmarks with the number of activities to be completed by certain dates. These sound like such simple steps, I know, but I'm just always surprised at how often kids don't know how to step themselves through that plan of looking at the big picture and then putting it down into smaller pieces . . . . It was really powerful to have the kids go in and see how many activities they had done. I started out with a chart, but I realized quickly that everybody wanted to keep track on their own. Some people wanted to write it in their planner, and some in a list. Some wanted to write it on a sticky note. They also had that reflective piece—they talked about the why. 'Why was I on task?' 'Why was I distracted?'"

—Julie, credit recovery facilitator

Outline of Instructional Activities

- **Initial Instruction:** Your goal is for students to be able to identify a variety of ways to monitor both progress and actions within efforts to self-regulate.

  - ➤ **Activity 26**—What Do You Monitor?
  - ➤ **Activity 27**—Taking Small Steps to Reach Big Goals
  - ➤ **Activity 28**—Monitoring Emotional Regulation
  - ➤ **Activity 29**—Monitoring Actions and Progress
  - ➤ **Activity 30**—Exploring Monitoring Methods
  - ➤ **Activity 31**—Check for Understanding

- **Guided Collaborative Learning:** Your goal is for students to be able to determine methods for monitoring actions and progress within situation-specific self-regulation planning.

  - ➤ **Activity 32**—Brainstorming Monitoring Options
  - ➤ **Activity 33**—What Do Athletes Monitor?
  - ➤ **Activity 34**—Is Anthony Saving Money?
  - ➤ **Activity 35**—Monitoring Olivia's Homework Plan
  - ➤ **Activity 36**—Is Levi's Anxiety Decreasing?
  - ➤ **Activity 37**—Situational Judgment Assessment

- **Independent Practice With Feedback:** Your goal is for students to design effective monitoring techniques for their endeavors.

  - ➤ **Activity 38**—Monitoring Your Short-Term Plan
  - ➤ **Activity 39**—Monitoring Your Effort and Learning
  - ➤ **Activity 40**—Monitoring Your Homework Completion

Initial Instruction

Through these activities, students learn critical concepts, make connections to their lives, and build a shared vocabulary. Your goal is for students to be able to identify a variety of ways to monitor both progress and actions within efforts to self-regulate.

Activity 26: What Do You Monitor?

Remind students that the second component of self-regulation is monitoring. The self-regulation poster (figure 1.2, page 20) illustrates the components. Using a think-pair-share technique, ask students to define the word *monitor*. After students have shared their definitions, display this definition.

Monitor: observe and check the progress or quality of something over a period of time; keep under systematic review.

Discuss similarities and differences between students' definitions and this definition; likely students included part of the definition (such as *observe* or *check*), but they may not have considered that monitoring is an ongoing or frequent behavior that is typically planned in advance.

Have students work as a class to generate a list of things that they currently monitor (such as grades, homework submission, project completion, performance in sports, progress in mastering a musical composition, money saved, and growth in an ability to do something). If students completed activity 3 (page 18), display this list of self-regulation examples and prompt students to add ways to monitor each example. Write down these ideas to reference in later activities.

Activity 27: Taking Small Steps to Reach Big Goals

Display the Tanzanian proverb, "Little by little, a little becomes a lot" (Ritualize, 2017). In small groups or as a whole class, discuss the following two prompts.

1. What does this quote mean?

2. How does it relate to self-regulation and progress toward goal attainment?

Emphasize that progress requires a series of many small steps. When monitoring, it is important that we track these small steps that lead toward the outcome. This helps us maintain our progress and not get discouraged when we don't immediately reach our goals. In small groups, prompt students to discuss a time when they weren't good at something, but through continued effort, they expanded their skills. This could be associated with learning a sport or a musical instrument, learning a concept in school, learning to ride a bike or drive a car, and so on. Emphasize that ongoing practice leads to progress and, in fact, strengthens neuropathways in our brains.

WHAT TEACHERS SAY

"I saw many improvements in each student without having to basically hold their hand and walk them through every step and every note of songs. Seeing the solo and ensemble kids rehearsing on their own and showing ownership seems to encourage more of the large ensemble students to come in for extra practice."

—Curtis, choir and band teacher

Activity 28: Monitoring Emotional Regulation

When it comes to regulating our emotional reactions, we often think about "what ifs" or wish we had reacted differently. This is only helpful if we use that reflection to more effectively monitor our emotions and then adjust our reactions in the future. As a group, discuss the idea of monitoring our emotions. How do you know when you are feeling anxiety or anger? What does it feel like; what are the physiological signs? Examples might include increased heart rate, feeling hot, hands or whole body feeling shaky or unsteady, clenched jaw, and shoulder tension.

Anger often hides other emotions. Return to the feeling words wheel in activity 15 (figure 2.1, page 38), and, in small groups, ask students to choose one word in the outside circle related to anger (like *embarrassed, jealous, irritated,* or *skeptical*) and discuss the similarities and differences between that feeling and anger. In a large group, ask students to share highlights from their discussions.

Explain to students that when you feel yourself becoming aggravated, you can use a calming technique or remove yourself from a situation without doing or saying something that you will later regret. Brainstorm ideas for monitoring emotions and the use of relaxation techniques. Examples might include a journal, chart, calendar, or rating scale.

WHAT TEACHERS SAY

"I have one student who missed so much school last year because he was really struggling with anxiety and didn't know how to regulate himself that way, and he was worried about assignments being due. And now our first quarter after using this program, he didn't have one missing assignment. He missed one day of school because he was sick, which was a vast improvement over what we saw last year. So that was a huge win for me."

—Laura, special education teacher

Activity 29: Monitoring Actions and Progress

Explain that we need to monitor *progress toward our goal* and monitor *our actions related to our plan*. For instance, if I wanted to improve my grade in English class, but the only thing I'm monitoring is my grade (the progress toward my goal), then I'm not going to have enough information to help me make effective changes to reach my goal. Being aware of my grade is one piece of the puzzle, but it's not the only thing I need to monitor. I also need to monitor the specific things that affect my grade. Am I regularly losing points for turning in late homework? Am I losing points because I'm not following instructions on assignments or because I'm not understanding the material? Am I losing points for talking in class or being tardy? These are actions that go into calculating my overall grade, and if I'm only checking on the grade and not analyzing how I'm doing on all those pieces, then I'm not going to be able to effectively identify and work on my problem areas, and I'm not likely to make progress toward improving my grade.

Return to the list of things students monitor from activity 26 (page 59). Working in small groups, have students categorize each monitoring option as *monitoring progress toward a goal* or *monitoring actions*. Some monitoring options may not fall clearly into a single category. Figure 3.1 provides examples of aligned progress and actions. If your students' lists include primarily progress indicators, encourage them to brainstorm and add actions that support their progress.

Monitoring Progress Toward a Goal: Am I improving?	Monitoring Actions: What am I doing to get there?
Grades	Checking off homework when completed
Healthy eating	Food diary entries
Timed one-mile run	Completing daily workouts
Amount of money saved	Categorizing all money spent

FIGURE 3.1: EXAMPLES FOR MONITORING PROGRESS AND ACTIONS.

Activity 30: Exploring Monitoring Methods

Explain that there are many strategies and tools, including technology, that we can use for monitoring our behavior, mood, nutrition, health habits, productivity, and so on. Break the class into eight small groups and assign one of the monitoring methods in figure 3.2 (page 62) to each group. Ask each group to come up with at least one example of when they might use the monitoring technique and describe why the monitoring technique works to help people stay on track toward a goal. Then have each group summarize their discussion for the whole class.

Monitoring Method	Description	Example	Why It Works
Graph or tallies	Documenting specific information at regular intervals, then using a graph to illustrate improvement		
Journal	Writing a brief entry each day that describes the progress you've made so far, barriers you've encountered, emotions that you are feeling, and specific actions for getting back on track		
Rubric	Comparing your work to the success criteria to see if you have met the standards and to figure out specific areas where you need to improve		
To-do list or checklist	Breaking larger tasks down into small pieces to make sure you don't miss anything, and checking off each piece as you complete it		
Timeline	Working backward from the overall due date to assign specific deadlines for each smaller piece, then regularly checking on whether you are meeting the smaller deadlines		
Repeated self-ratings or self-assessments	Regularly reflecting on your effort, learning, or emotions and reactions by giving yourself a score at various intervals, and then reviewing the ratings to determine your progress across time		
Video or picture log	Documenting progress in a visual format to display improvement over time		
Accountability partner meetings	Having someone check in on you periodically to see if you are on target and to discuss any adjustment you might need to make to reach your goal		

FIGURE 3.2: MONITORING METHODS.

Visit go.SolutionTree.com/SEL for a free reproducible version of this figure.

WHAT TEACHERS SAY

"Time is actually on their mind. I hear them in their discussions talking about when certain assignments are due. They are looking forward to the final assignment, and they're already talking about their plan and their sketch that is going to be due soon. They were explaining to each other how they would have more time to work with the clay if they complete their plan at home over break. I'm really happy with what I'm seeing so far."

—Panthea, art teacher

Activity 31: Check for Understanding

Using response cards or an online quiz platform, gather individual students' responses to the items displayed in figure 3.3. Review the responses to ensure that students understand the concept of monitoring. Reteach as necessary. [The answer key for figure 3.3 is: 1–actions; 2–progress; 3–actions; 4–d.]

Monitoring Progress or Actions

Your goal is to get eight hours of sleep each night. Categorize the following monitoring techniques as either monitoring progress toward the goal or monitoring actions.

1. _____ Using a calendar to write down the time you went to bed

2. _____ Graphing the number of hours you slept each night

3. _____ Using a log to describe your evening activities and how they may have influenced your sleep

Multiple Choice

4. Which of these would you NOT use to monitor your self-regulation?

   a. A graph showing your progress over time

   b. A journal where you describe daily progress and identify whether you are on track with your original plan

   c. A rubric to compare with your work to see if you are meeting the criteria

   d. A comparison of your progress to your friend's progress on the same project or assignment

---

FIGURE 3.3: CHECK FOR UNDERSTANDING—MONITORING PROGRESS AND ACTIONS.

*Visit **go.SolutionTree.com/SEL** for a free reproducible version of this figure.*

Guided Collaborative Learning

Scenario-based activities address an array of circumstances to which adolescents can relate. Through these collaborative-learning activities, students gain a deeper understanding of self-regulation concepts. Your goal is for students to be able to determine methods for monitoring actions and progress within situation-specific self-regulation planning.

Activity 32: Brainstorming Monitoring Options

Have students brainstorm options for the goals outlined in figure 3.4, discussing ideas for monitoring both progress toward the goal and the specific actions that impact this progress. If students have already generated monitoring options for one of these goals in a previous activity, add scenarios that are relevant to your students. Review the example together.

Self-Regulation Goal	Monitoring Progress Toward the Goal: Am I improving?	Monitoring Actions: What am I doing to get there?
Example: **Getting to school on time** Part of my plan includes going to bed at a specific time each night and setting an extra alarm.	Using my calendar to note the days I get to school on time	• Tracking bedtime on the calendar, including reasons for late bedtimes • Tally of the number of times the alarm went off before I got up • Daily journaling—if I felt well rested, if there were things that affected my punctuality (such as not gathering my school stuff until that morning) • Reviewing my journal and calendar together to determine changes to make to my plan
1. **Running in a 5K in two months** My plan includes getting adequate nutrition, running daily, and setting distance and time goals for each week.		
2. **Improving my mastery of mathematics concepts** My plan includes studying an extra half hour each night and doing well on the concept quizzes.		
3. **Reducing my anxiety before tests by using calming techniques** My plan includes trying different techniques to determine the most effective ones.		
4. **Increasing my speed in swimming the 100-meter breaststroke** My plan includes daily swimming and weightlifting.		
5. **Writing a quality research paper** My plan includes finding ten sources, outlining each paragraph, and reviewing the rubric.		

FIGURE 3.4: DETERMINING OPTIONS FOR MONITORING PROGRESS AND ACTIONS.

Visit **go.SolutionTree.com/SEL** *for a free reproducible version of this figure.*

WHAT STUDENTS SAY

"For big projects, I use a checklist to keep track of what I've done. I make percentages out of my checklist to put my progress into number form."

—Twelfth-grade student

Activity 33: What Do Athletes Monitor?

In small groups, have students select an athlete, such as LeBron James, and create a list of fitness actions and progress indicators that the athlete likely monitors. Most famous athletes have been interviewed numerous times about their fitness routine and diet, so finding information online usually isn't too difficult. Prompt groups to create a two-column chart identifying progress indicators and actions that the athlete likely monitors. For example, in the progress column for LeBron, students could include monitoring his free-throw percentage, while in the action column they might include shooting free throws for thirty minutes each day. Another example might include progress in the height that he can jump, while the actions would include the number of power skipping repetitions completed during daily training. Have groups share interesting findings with the whole class.

Activity 34: Is Anthony Saving Money?

Let's return to Anthony's money-saving scenario (activity 20, page 43). Don't worry if you didn't use the prior activity; the following scenario provides all the information needed for this activity. This scenario is reproducible from appendix C (page 163).

SCENARIO

Anthony wants to save money for a gaming system. He has a part-time job and makes about $80 per week. Anthony usually spends all his money going out to eat with friends. Anthony knows that he's going to need to use self-regulation to save the money for the gaming system.

As a class, discuss the following questions to brainstorm ideas for monitoring.

- What should Anthony monitor?
- How might he monitor both his progress and his actions?
- How often will Anthony need to monitor?

For example, Anthony should monitor the amount of money he has saved (progress), but he should also categorize the money he spends and determine whether the purchase was necessary or could possibly be avoided in the future (actions). He could also monitor ways he and his friends hang out that don't require money (actions). Anthony might even monitor what he buys when he goes out to eat, determining the cheapest options (actions).

Wrap up the discussion by asking students to compare steps that they take to save money with Anthony's approach. Remind students that our monitoring techniques vary depending on our goal and our personal challenges in reaching the goal. While Anthony frequently spends money on food, we each may have different challenges to saving money, and therefore what and how we monitor will also be unique.

Activity 35: Monitoring Olivia's Homework Plan

Give students a few minutes to review the plan that they made to help Olivia with homework completion (activity 21, page 44) or use the example plan provided in the same activity. Then provide the following scenario, also reproducible from appendix C (page 163).

SCENARIO

Olivia has been using the self-regulation plan for homework completion for two weeks now. She has been doing some monitoring. She checks off assignments that she turned in on time, and she uses the list to calculate her percentage of on-time homework—she is at 80 percent now, up from 50 percent before the plan. She can tell from comparing her first percentage to her current one that she has improved a lot, but she wants to improve further. The problem is that Olivia is not sure where she is getting off track, so she is asking you to help her figure it out. You know that to do this, she will have to expand her focus from just monitoring her percentage of assignments completed on time to include monitoring specific actions, so you decide to help her brainstorm how to expand her monitoring.

After giving students time to read the scenario, have them work in groups to come up with specific things they could monitor for homework completion, including how often each piece needs to be monitored. Use these guiding questions as necessary to help students identify what and how to monitor.

Are you tracking whether you are . . .

- Recording your assignments accurately and in detail?
- Gathering all the necessary materials from school and taking them home?
- Starting homework at a specific time?

- Managing your after-school time effectively?

- Getting out the supplies you need when you start working on homework?

- Managing distractions effectively?

- Asking for help or reviewing material when you don't understand something?

- Checking your homework for accuracy?

- Completing the homework?

- Putting your homework in your backpack after you completed it and remembering to turn it in?

Prompt groups to share their monitoring examples. Wrap up the discussion by reminding students that, while monitoring progress toward a goal is part of the process, it is not the only piece. We also need to make a habit of regularly monitoring our actions because without that knowledge, we won't necessarily be able to tell what part of our plan is tripping us up when we encounter problems or aren't making as much progress as we expected.

WHAT TEACHERS SAY

"Students seemed less overwhelmed when they monitored their progress one lesson at a time as opposed to viewing a chapter as a large, all-encompassing entity. They were able to make concrete plans in order to stay proactive instead of reactive when dealing with deadlines. I think this improved students' confidence and organization."

—*Jarrod, mathematics teacher*

Activity 36: Is Levi's Anxiety Decreasing?

Discuss monitoring techniques for Levi's public speaking plan by sharing the following scenario and figure 3.5 (page 68). The scenario is also referenced in activity 22 (page 46) and in activity 59 (page 105) and is reproducible from appendix C (page 163). As a class, determine what Levi could monitor. Write down the ideas as students share them. The ideas should address whether he is completing each step in his plan, how prepared he feels for the speech, emotions that he is feeling, and the effectiveness of the self-calming techniques. Then in small groups, have students brainstorm how Levi could monitor each piece and when this monitoring would occur.

SCENARIO

Your friend, Levi, is taking a public speaking class. He knows that he will be expected to speak in front of groups in the career he plans to pursue. The only problem is that Levi gets very anxious when

Levi's Public Speaking Plan

- Seven days before speech
  - Finish writing the speech.
- Six days before speech
  - Read the speech silently four times.
  - Read the speech aloud twice, taking three deep breaths prior to each reading.
- Five days before speech
  - Read the speech aloud twice, taking three deep breaths prior to each reading.
  - Write bulleted notes to use when giving the speech.
  - Practice the first half of the speech with only the bulleted notes.
  - Envision classmates smiling as they listen to the speech.
- Four days before speech
  - Practice the first half of the speech with only the bulleted notes; refer to full speech when needed; take three deep breaths prior to each practice.
  - Read second half of speech aloud twice.
  - Practice the second half of the speech with only the bulleted notes.
  - Envision classmates smiling as they listen to the speech.
- Three days before speech
  - Practice entire speech with only bulleted notes, keep practicing until confident, and focus on speaking clearly and slowly.
  - Record the whole speech and then watch the video to determine areas that need more practice.
  - Reflect on mastery of speech. Use positive self-talk ("I am prepared for the speech. I can do this!") to increase confidence.
  - Give the speech to a family member; ask for feedback on tone and pace.
  - Using the feedback, practice the entire speech a few more times, taking deep breaths prior to each practice.
- Two days before speech
  - Record the whole speech and then watch the video to determine areas that need more practice.
  - Practice the speech aloud, envisioning the classmates who will be watching.
  - Pause at key break points and repeat a mental reminder to slow down and speak clearly.
  - Give the speech to a family member or friend.
- Day before speech
  - Take deep breaths and then practice the speech, envisioning the classmates who will be watching.
  - Pause at key break points and repeat a mental reminder to slow down and speak clearly.
  - Repeat the mantra: "I'm prepared for the speech. I can do this!"
- Day of speech
  - Practice the speech once.
  - If possible, volunteer to go first.
  - Take three deep breaths before giving the speech and think, "I am prepared for the speech. I can do this!"
  - Talk slowly and clearly; make eye contact if comfortable or look just slightly over their heads if nervous.
  - Pause at key break points to take a breath and repeat a mental reminder to talk slowly and clearly.
  - Finish the speech and reflect on effort and positive outcomes.

FIGURE 3.5: LEVI'S PUBLIC SPEAKING PLAN.

*Visit **go.SolutionTree.com/SEL** for a free reproducible version of this figure.*

speaking in front of a group. His palms sweat and his mouth gets very dry. He ends up talking too fast and without emotion. Help Levi monitor his plan for reducing his anxiety and effectively conveying his ideas to a group.

Have each student pair up with another student who wasn't in his or her group. Each student should share three monitoring techniques that Levi could use. Switch partners and repeat the sharing two more times. Then have students return to their groups and discuss additional monitoring options that they heard.

Activity 37: Situational Judgment Assessment

Ask students to independently read the scenario and answer the prompt. This scenario extends through each chapter, building on prior answers. A reproducible form with all situational judgment assessments is provided in appendix A (page 153).

SCENARIO

In health class, Alex and his classmates learned about the benefits of drinking an adequate amount of water each day. Alex has decided that he does not drink enough water.

Determine when and how Alex will monitor his progress and actions throughout each day.

Review each student's answers to determine whether the monitoring methods include both progress (water consumption) and numerous actions (such as bringing water to school and drinking water at key intervals throughout the day).

Independent Practice With Feedback

Through independent practice, students begin applying their learning to their own endeavors. This promotes fluency in use of the skills and provides opportunities for formative feedback and coaching. Your goal is for students to design effective monitoring techniques for their personal and academic efforts.

Activity 38: Monitoring Your Short-Term Plan

Prompt students to individually review the plan they made in activity 24 (page 49) or activity 25 (page 51), and write a brief summary of the plan, what things (if any) they've been monitoring so far, and new ideas for monitoring now that they've learned more about how to do it. Remind students that monitoring needs to focus on both progress and specific actions that lead to this progress. Referring to figure 3.2 (page 62), prompt students to determine which monitoring techniques they have incorporated: graphs or tallies, journal entries, rubrics, to-do lists or checklists, timelines, repeated self-ratings or self-assessments, video or picture logs, or accountability partner meetings.

Then have students work with a partner to review and provide feedback on each other's ideas for monitoring progress and actions. When giving each other feedback, students can reflect on the questions outlined in figure 3.6. Encourage students to take notes on their partner's suggestions and update monitoring techniques based on the feedback.

Feedback Prompts for Monitoring

1. Are you monitoring progress toward the outcome?

2. Are you monitoring specific actions that impact progress?

3. Which monitoring techniques have you included? How might you add other techniques?

    - Graphs or tallies: Documenting specific information at regular intervals, and then using a graph to illustrate improvement

    - Journal: Writing a brief entry each day that describes the progress you've made so far, barriers you've encountered, emotions you are feeling, and specific actions for getting back on track

    - Rubric: Comparing your work to the success criteria to see if you have met the standards and to figure out specific areas where you need to improve

    - To-do list or checklist: Breaking larger tasks down into small pieces to make sure you don't miss anything, and checking off each piece as you complete it

    - Timeline: Working backward from the due date to assign specific deadlines for each smaller piece, then regularly checking on whether you are meeting the smaller deadlines

    - Repeated self-ratings or self-assessments: Regularly reflecting on your effort, learning, or emotions and reactions by giving yourself a score at various intervals, and then reviewing the ratings to determine your progress across time

    - Video or picture log: Documenting progress in a visual format to display improvement over time

    - Accountability partner meetings: Having someone check in on you periodically to see if you are on target and to discuss any adjustment you might need to make to reach your goal

4. When will monitoring occur? How will the information be documented for review later?

FIGURE 3.6: FEEDBACK PROMPTS FOR MONITORING.

*Visit **go.SolutionTree.com/SEL** for a free reproducible version of this figure.*

Have each student finalize and submit a list of monitoring techniques. Provide feedback to each student, commenting on positive aspects and providing specific suggestions. Prompt students to enact their monitoring techniques. In the next chapter, students will learn how to adjust their plans based on their monitoring data.

Activity 39: Monitoring Your Effort and Learning

Show students figure 3.7 and explain that they can use this chart to monitor actions and progress. Have students read the two columns to determine which one monitors progress toward the goal of mastering a challenging concept (the answer is *learning*) and which monitors actions (the answer is *effort*).

Challenging learning task:		
(1 = Low level of effort and learning; 5 = High level of effort and learning)		
Effort	↕	**Learning**
5. I tried very hard and kept a growth mindset. My effort is helping me learn.		5. I know this so well that I could explain it to others.
4. I tried hard and kept a growth mindset, but distractions sometimes got in the way. I will work to maintain my focus.		4. I can get the right answer, but I don't know it well enough to explain it to others yet.
3. I tried even when I got frustrated, but there is more I could do. I will work to keep a growth mindset and focus my efforts.		3. I understand most of this, but I have more to learn.
2. I tried but got frustrated and gave up quickly. I will focus on how mistakes are part of learning.		2. I understand some of this, but I have a lot more to learn.
1. I didn't really try to learn. I will put in more effort.		1. I do not understand this yet.

Source: © 2019 by Amy Gaumer Erickson and Patricia Noonan. Used with permission.

FIGURE 3.7: EFFORT AND LEARNING CHART.

*Visit **go.SolutionTree.com/SEL** for a free reproducible version of this figure.*

Individually, have students think of a challenging assignment or concept that they have just started working on (preferably in your class). Prompt students to write their selected learning task in the first row of figure 3.7, then draw a line between the statements that best describe how they're feeling about their effort and learning on this task so far. Discuss the following questions as a class.

- What is the relationship between effort and learning?

- Can you put in a lot of effort but still be at the bottom of the learning column?

- If you are at the top of the learning column, do you still need to put in a lot of effort?

Wrap up the discussion by explaining that effort and learning go together, but they aren't the same thing. Sometimes we have to put in a lot of effort to make progress in learning, and for other things, we might not need to put in much effort at all.

Ask students how they could use the effort and learning chart to monitor their actions and progress. Extend the activity by prompting students on multiple occasions to use this chart to measure their effort and learning as they make progress toward mastering a new concept or skill. Prior to a test or quiz, ask students to reflect on their effort and learning, as well as the relationship between the two.

WHAT TEACHERS SAY

"Make sure to distinguish between action and progress. Many times, the kids I work with don't see the difference. I utilize the Effort and Learning Chart as a way to prompt students to monitor their daily progress at intervention time. I also have them mark what zone [feeling and level of energy] they feel they were in during interventions."

—Jane, special education teacher

Activity 40: Monitoring Your Homework Completion

Show students the homework log in figure 3.8 and challenge them to use it over the next week to monitor their own homework efforts. Remind students that while this tool is a good way to get started, their monitoring should involve more than just these pieces. It should monitor such things as whether the workspace was effective and how distractions were managed. This is a tool to help them get started and make monitoring a part of their daily process.

After one week of use, discuss the results with students. What did they notice? How did the log help them? Were there aspects that were challenging, such as remembering to use the log or estimating the time needed to complete an assignment? Extend the activity by encouraging students to modify the log items and format to better meet their needs, then continue to use the log for monitoring.

WHAT STUDENTS SAY

"I'm the type of person that leaves everything to the last minute. Now I will do this less . . . . I saw that this week I was getting my work done, not only for this class but for my precalculus class as well. When I made my plan and wrote it on paper, I then monitored my work. I took control of my assignments and was able to finish everything on time."

—Eleventh-grade student

Planning				Monitoring Actions			Monitoring Progress	
Class and Assignment	Do I have all the materials?	Estimated difficulty (1 = Easy; 5 = Hard) Do I need help?	Do I need to break it into smaller pieces? If yes, add rows.	Estimated time needed to complete	Actual time to complete	Actual difficulty (1 = Easy; 5 = Hard)	Effort (1 = Low; 5 = High)	Anticipated grade	Actual grade

Source: © 2019 by Amy Gaumer Erickson and Patricia Noonan. Used with permission.

FIGURE 3.8: HOMEWORK LOG.

Visit go.SolutionTree.com/SEL for a free reproducible version of this figure.

Summary

These instructional activities promote students' understanding of monitoring techniques and the purpose of monitoring both actions and progress toward an outcome. The reproducible instructional planning tool provides a guide for planning your instruction. Students will continue to gain proficiency in monitoring through ongoing practice that includes prompting and feedback. Through monitoring, students connect their actions to the desired outcome, increasing their self-efficacy through the conscious documentation of their growth.

Determine whether you will customize the vignettes or adapt activities to resonate with your students. Then consider how you could provide ongoing practice and feedback to students. Select instructional activities that will help your students meet the initial instruction, guided collaborative learning, and independent practice learning targets.

Monitoring Your Plan and Progress

INSTRUCTIONAL PLANNING TOOL

Initial Instruction: Students identify a variety of ways to monitor both progress and actions within efforts to self-regulate.	
Instructional Activities	Notes and Adaptations
Activity 26: What Do You Monitor?	
Activity 27: Taking Small Steps to Reach Big Goals	
Activity 28: Monitoring Emotional Regulation	
Activity 29: Monitoring Actions and Progress	
Activity 30: Exploring Monitoring Methods	
Activity 31: Check for Understanding	

Guided Collaborative Learning: Students determine methods for monitoring actions and progress within situation-specific self-regulation planning.	
Instructional Activities	Notes and Adaptations
Activity 32: Brainstorming Monitoring Options	
Activity 33: What Do Athletes Monitor?	
Activity 34: Is Anthony Saving Money?	
Activity 35: Monitoring Olivia's Homework Plan	
Activity 36: Is Levi's Anxiety Decreasing?	
Activity 37: Situational Judgment Assessment	

Independent Practice With Feedback: Students design effective monitoring techniques for their endeavors.	
Instructional Activities	Notes and Adaptations
Activity 38: Monitoring Your Short-Term Plan	
Activity 39: Monitoring Your Effort and Learning	
Activity 40: Monitoring Your Homework Completion	

How will you provide ongoing practice addressing each learning target?

When and how can you provide feedback to each student?

CHAPTER 4

ADJUSTING YOUR PLAN

We regularly encounter obstacles and make midcourse corrections when things don't go according to plan. This moment of hitting a roadblock can stall our efforts if we don't know how to manage distractions and overcome obstacles. Self-regulating includes thinking through which strategies will be most effective in helping you reach your goal while still being realistic about the other demands on your time, attention, and energy. Effective techniques for managing distractions and overcoming barriers include removing temptations from sight (Duckworth, White, Matteucci, Shearer, & Gross, 2016), mentally contrasting your choices with the consequences of each choice (Gollwitzer, Oettingen, Kirby, Duckworth, & Mayer, 2011), and determining implementation intentions by writing out if–then plans that proactively outline the actions to take if you encounter specific barriers (Gollwitzer, 1999; Guderjahn, Gold, Stadler, & Gawrilow, 2013). Adjustments occur throughout the enactment of our self-regulation plans; although needed adjustments are sometimes unexpected, they can often be identified in advance with careful consideration of potential barriers and corresponding corrective actions.

WHAT TEACHERS SAY

"I've seen an increase not only in participation, I've noticed that students are taking this seriously, and they are feeling more aware of who they are and what they can accomplish, big or small."

—Hanna, language arts teacher

We make adjustments as a result of monitoring and realizing that we are off track, but monitoring alone does not tell us what adjustments should be made. For example, if a student is monitoring his grades and notices that he has numerous missing assignments, he has become more self-aware of a problem, but he might not know how to overcome it. At this point, he will need to reflect on his actions and possibly brainstorm with another person about how to adjust his homework plan for not only completing the missing assignments but also for completing upcoming assignments in a timely manner. While it is tempting to tell students what to do to succeed, it is more beneficial to work with students to build their capacity by asking questions that promote problem solving and increase the likelihood that they will initiate meaningful modifications.

Now let's return to Mrs. Cooper's class and the progress of the research project.

Mrs. Cooper's Research Project

Everything has been progressing smoothly in the research project. Students are meeting in small groups with others who are using the same monitoring technique. In these groups, Mrs. Cooper hears students talk about challenges and distractions, brainstorming together on how these can be addressed. She prompts students to write down the adjustments they are going to make.

Students have been talking about interesting lab work they've been doing in science, and Mrs. Cooper starts thinking about the similarities between experiments and self-regulation adjustments. She asks the class if they see commonalities. They mention trying different techniques, judging the effectiveness of their strategies, determining the best course of action, and adding to their plans. She then shows students the Thomas Edison quote, "I have not failed. I have just found 10,000 ways that won't work" (Mallory, 2012). Together they discuss how adjusting self-regulation plans is like conducting experiments—both require some trial and error, as well as learning from prior attempts to make each attempt more successful.

While students are working independently on their research papers, Mrs. Cooper conducts five-minute conferences with each student. "Tell me about your progress," is all she says to begin each conference. Mrs. Cooper is amazed at the details this prompt elicits. Students show her their self-regulation plans with numerous tasks checked off, modifications outlined, and next steps highlighted. They talk about adjustments they have made, such as adding in more time a couple evenings each week to work on the research or keeping all research in a notebook that is easy to transport in their backpack. Mrs. Cooper then asks, "What other challenges are you encountering?" Mrs. Cooper notes the challenges encountered and brainstorms solutions with each student.

> After the conferences, Mrs. Cooper reviews all the challenges that students are encountering and determines two connected themes: finding reputable sources and citing them correctly. She decides to provide further instruction and facilitate students' discussions around these topics.

When students adjust their actions in response to monitoring data, they better manage distractions, overcome obstacles, and take ownership over their learning. Through this self-appraisal process, students remedy discrepancies between their efforts and the desired outcomes (Frey et al., 2018). In simpler terms, when students think about what they are doing and how they are progressing, they identify adjustments that lead to greater success. The instructional activities in this chapter are designed to increase students' ability to anticipate barriers, analyze options, and determine a course of action that maintains their focus on the desired outcome.

Outline of Instructional Activities

- **Initial Instruction:** Your goal is for students to acknowledge that everyone faces obstacles and that it is possible to overcome those obstacles by adjusting their efforts.

  - ➤ **Activity 41**—Reflecting on Past Obstacles

  - ➤ **Activity 42**—Famous People on Overcoming Obstacles

  - ➤ **Activity 43**—Is Your Phone a Tool or Distraction?

  - ➤ **Activity 44**—Mental Contrasting

  - ➤ **Activity 45**—Check for Understanding

- **Guided Collaborative Learning:** Your goal is for students to be able to anticipate common obstacles and determine adjustments for specific situations.

  - ➤ **Activity 46**—Anthony Gets Off Track While Saving Money

  - ➤ **Activity 47**—Connecting Barriers and Strategies

  - ➤ **Activity 48**—Writing If–Then Statements

  - ➤ **Activity 49**—Making Choices That Work for You

  - ➤ **Activity 50**—Situational Judgment Assessment

- **Independent Practice With Feedback:** Your goal is for students to evaluate their monitoring efforts to determine if their plans are off track, identify any obstacles that are derailing them, determine specific actions and strategies to get back on track, and incorporate the new actions into their future monitoring efforts.

Initial Instruction

Through these activities, students learn critical self-regulation concepts, make connections to their lives, and build a shared vocabulary. Your goal is for students to acknowledge that everyone faces obstacles and that it is possible to overcome those obstacles by adjusting their efforts.

Activity 41: Reflecting on Past Obstacles

Explain the third component of self-regulation: adjust as needed when things are not going as planned. Everyone faces obstacles and setbacks, but instead of getting discouraged and giving up, we can use these setbacks to improve our self-regulation going forward. Remind students that the "self" part of self-regulation means that *you* have to regulate your own actions and that this component focuses on the process of taking ownership of your effort and learning (rather than relying on parents, teachers, or friends to tell you what to do). To simplify, only *you* truly know the best way to help *you*. Others can brainstorm with you, but it won't be as meaningful or effective unless you're the one making the final decision.

Acknowledge that one of the reasons we sometimes give up or fail when something doesn't go according to our plan is that we can't see where we got off course, and even if we do, we might still not know what to do to get back on track. What we learned about monitoring (chapter 3, page 55) helps us identify *how* we are getting derailed. Next, we have to determine *why* our plan was unsuccessful in order to identify specific ways to address those issues and continue making progress toward our goals. Explain that if we consider things in advance that could potentially block our progress, then we can incorporate ways to avoid those obstacles from the outset.

Provide an example from your own life of a time you initiated a plan but the plan was disrupted or left unfinished. Use these questions to explain how you could have adjusted your plan.

- What specifically derailed my plan?

- What specific actions could I have taken to get back on track?

- What resources (including assistance from other people) could I have used to get back on track?

- What consequences or rewards could I have given myself along the way to support my progress?

Ask students to think about times they have given up before reaching a goal. Were you saving money for something you really wanted? Did you quit playing a sport after you got cut from a team? Did you decide that playing a musical instrument wasn't for you? Did you quit an exercise plan after you got sick? Did you stop playing a game because you couldn't get to the next level? Did you move out of an honors course because it was really challenging? Emphasize that sometimes our goals or interests change, but more often we give up because the task is more challenging than we anticipated, or we get frustrated when we don't succeed right away.

Next, ask students to think about a time when something was challenging, but they succeeded. In pairs, prompt students to discuss these three questions.

1. What obstacles did you have to overcome?

2. How did you encourage yourself to keep going?

3. How did you adjust your efforts to succeed?

Ask for volunteers to share with the class. Emphasize that we have all encountered obstacles and given up on our plans at some point, but by focusing on adjusting our plans, we can continue to make progress despite the obstacles.

Activity 42: Famous People on Overcoming Obstacles

Divide students into six small groups and assign each group one of the following quotes about overcoming obstacles (you can add other quotes or find song lyrics that are relevant for your students). In their groups, have students discuss what the quote means and how it relates to self-regulation, and then report out to the class on their group's conclusions.

- "The real glory is being knocked to your knees and then coming back." —Vince Lombardi (BrainyQuote, n.d.c)

- "You may encounter many defeats, but you must not be defeated. In fact, it may be necessary to encounter the defeats, so you can know who you are, what you can rise from, how you can still come out of it." —Maya Angelou (Goodreads, n.d.b)

- "It's not that I'm so smart, it's just that I stay with problems longer." —Albert Einstein (BrainyQuote, n.d.a)

- "A failure is not always a mistake. It may simply be the best one can do under the circumstances. The real mistake is to stop trying." —B. F. Skinner (Cherry, 2020)

- "Obstacles don't have to stop you. If you run into a wall, don't turn around and give up. Figure out how to climb it, go through it, or work around it." —Michael Jordan (BrainyQuote, n.d.b)

- "A hero is an ordinary individual who finds the strength to persevere and endure in spite of overwhelming obstacles." —Christopher Reeve (Wilderotter, 2014)

Wrap up the discussion by telling students that, as we work on our self-regulation in a variety of areas, there will be times when maintaining progress is very challenging. Remind them that self-regulation also involves building our *self-efficacy* (our belief in our ability to accomplish challenging tasks), strengthening our *perseverance* (our drive to keep working toward our goal despite setbacks), and improving our *adaptability* and *problem-solving* skills. A common misconception holds that people who accomplish big goals don't encounter obstacles along the way. On the contrary, they often do, but they have strategies to reflect, revise, get back on course, and continue making progress. In short, we are going to encounter obstacles and setbacks, but we don't have to let that stop us; instead, we can adjust as needed and keep moving forward.

WHAT STUDENTS SAY

"To get back up after being knocked down is the same as adjusting your plan. You get back up with a new tactic and try again."

—Twelfth-grade student

Activity 43: Is Your Phone a Tool or Distraction?

We can all agree that smartphones and similar devices are both productive tools and unproductive distractions for adults and adolescents. Start the conversation by asking students what annoys them about other people's phone use. Their answers may include things like parents not listening because they are looking at something on their phones, teammates not doing their fair share of work because they are on their phones, friends on their phones instead of doing something fun together, and people not paying attention when walking down the hallway.

Then make a T-chart, asking students to work in small groups to create a list of examples for using a phone as a productive tool as opposed to an unproductive distraction. Start by having students think about schoolwork, and then broaden the conversation to include sports and social interactions. An example is provided in figure 4.1. Students are likely to note that phone uses could fall in both columns, in which case it is fine to include the examples twice.

Productive Tool	Unproductive Distraction
Calculator	Games
Calendar	Social media
Communication tool	Constant notifications
Look up research	Shopping apps
See weather and news	Smart watch notifications
Access to grades and assignments	
Timer and stopwatch	
Camera	

FIGURE 4.1: SMARTPHONE USES.

Once the T-chart is made, discuss as a class how the unproductive distractions could be managed while still being able to use the smartphone as a tool. This might include closing apps, putting phones in airplane mode, or turning off notifications.

While we can't regulate for other people, we can work together to point out distractions and remind ourselves to self-regulate. Ask students, "What could you say to a friend who is distracted by her phone instead of paying attention to your conversation?" Remind students to be kind and limit their sarcasm. Write down a few of these phrases to potentially display when students are working in groups. Sample phrases include the following.

- "I know you are waiting for an important text, but I'd like to work on the activity with you."

- "You seem distracted by your phone; is it critical or could it wait?"

- "Can you look up information on your phone?"

- "Let's stay in the moment and put our phones away."

Activity 44: Mental Contrasting

Explain to students that a benefit of improving our self-regulation is that we also improve our ability to manage distractions and stay motivated toward achieving our goals. People who use a strategy called *mental contrasting* are more likely to reach their goals (Gollwitzer et al., 2011). Ask students to think about a goal or aspiration, then close their eyes and imagine all the good things that will come if they achieve their goal. Give students a minute to consider this, then ask them to imagine all the hurdles they might encounter on the way toward their goal and imagine themselves overcoming these hurdles (Oettingen, 2014). These steps are displayed in figure 4.2 (page 84).

Mental Contrasting Steps

1. Think about your goal.

2. Imagine all the good things that will come from achieving your goal.

3. Think about all the hurdles you might encounter on the way toward your goal.

4. Imagine overcoming these hurdles.

FIGURE 4.2: MENTAL CONTRASTING STEPS.

Explain to students that we all feel frustrated and sometimes feel like giving up on our goals. This strategy reminds us of why we want to achieve our goals and helps keep us motivated. Some people use this strategy every day. In a class discussion, ask students when they might use mental contrasting.

WHAT TEACHERS SAY

"The biggest improvement that I noticed in the short period of time that I have been teaching self-regulation is the 'monitor your progress' and 'adjust your plan' portions of the process. Many students see the beginning and the ending of a project, a week, or a test. To actually have them reflect on their plan and make changes to help them to meet their goal, that was fun to watch."

—*Stacia, English language arts teacher*

Activity 45: Check for Understanding

Using response cards or an online quiz platform, have students individually identify the component for each behavior displayed in figure 4.3. Review the responses to ensure that students understand the first three components of self-regulation. Reteach as necessary. [The answer key for figure 4.3 is: 1–monitor; 2–adjust; 3–plan; 4–adjust; 5–monitor.]

Identify which self-regulation component each behavior addresses.			
Behavior	**Component**		
1. Each day, crossing tasks off a to-do list as they are finished	Plan	Monitor	Adjust
2. Recognizing when something isn't working and immediately changing your plan to get back on track	Plan	Monitor	Adjust
3. Breaking down big goals into smaller pieces	Plan	Monitor	Adjust
4. After encountering setbacks, looking for solutions (and trying as many as needed) until you succeed	Plan	Monitor	Adjust
5. Identifying and using specific ways to track progress	Plan	Monitor	Adjust

FIGURE 4.3: CHECK FOR UNDERSTANDING—PLANNING, MONITORING, AND ADJUSTING.

Visit go.SolutionTree.com/SEL for a free reproducible version of this figure.

Guided Collaborative Learning

Scenario-based activities address an array of circumstances to which adolescents can relate. Through these collaborative-learning activities, students gain a deeper understanding of self-regulation concepts. Your goal is for students to be able to anticipate common obstacles and determine adjustments for specific situations.

Activity 46: Anthony Gets Off Track While Saving Money

Let's return to Anthony's money-saving scenario (activity 20, page 43, and activity 34, page 65). Don't worry if you didn't use the prior activities; the scenario below provides all the information you need for this activity. This scenario is reproducible from appendix C (page 163).

SCENARIO

Anthony is trying to save money for a gaming system. He has a part-time job and makes about $80 per week. Following his plan, Anthony has started hanging out with friends at their houses and is going out to eat far less. This is working to save money. However, during breaks at work, Anthony is buying snacks and a soda from the vending machine. He hadn't thought about this when he made his plan, but these snacks are cutting into his savings. How can Anthony adjust his plan?

In small groups, have students discuss options for how Anthony could adjust his plan to be more successful in saving money. Tell them that it's not enough to have Anthony bring snacks from home. They should think through how he will ensure the snacks are available at home, how he will remember to pack these snacks, and how he will track his progress and actions.

Bring the class back together, asking each group to share one action or step their group identified without repeating the action identified by a previous group. Elicit round-robin responses until all groups have shared the actions they identified. Wrap up the activity by acknowledging the creative thinking among the groups and encourage students to be creative when they are working to overcome their own obstacles.

Activity 47: Connecting Barriers and Strategies

There are many strategies to help students overcome barriers. As a class, review the example scenario in figure 4.4 (page 87). Then ask for volunteers to share other strategies that might help Lea. For example, for the second barrier of having things that she wants to do apart from exercising, Lea could determine alternate times to exercise if something else comes up, or she could tell her friends about her exercise plan and encourage them to join her.

Have students read scenarios 1 and 2 in figure 4.4 and individually identify two barriers the person may encounter and one strategy for addressing each barrier. Then, in small groups, have students discuss their answers, adding new ideas from the group. Because situations are complex, and there are many factors that contribute to self-regulation, there will likely be several answers that fit. Students should be able to explain why they chose a specific barrier and corresponding strategy.

Debrief with the class by reminding students that there are many options for overcoming barriers, and it is often helpful to discuss barriers with others to come up with creative solutions. Remind students that the best way to overcome obstacles is to imagine in advance what might go wrong and then plan for contingencies, but this isn't always possible. By regularly monitoring, you will be aware of when you get off course. The key is to adjust quickly by modifying your plan or working around an obstacle. One of the biggest benefits of self-regulation is that it helps you be more proactive and get better at recognizing and addressing your mistakes on your own rather than waiting for someone else to point them out and suggest how to fix them. Of course, it is a good idea to ask others to brainstorm solutions with you. If you've recognized that you have a problem and aren't sure how to fix it, by asking someone to brainstorm with you, you are taking ownership of your progress and taking the first step to address the issue.

WHAT TEACHERS SAY

"I think my students have benefited in their ownership of the weights program! I see more of my students working harder while in the weight room and asking what they can be doing on their own to reach their goals."

—Stephanie, physical education teacher

Activity 48: Writing If–Then Statements

Explain that we can anticipate and plan for obstacles in advance through a strategy called implementation intentions (Gollwitzer, 1999). Using the scenarios in figure 4.5 (page 88), prompt students to brainstorm potential obstacles and write if–then statements to strategize how to address specific complications: *if* this happens, *then* I will do this. As a class, review the example provided. Create jigsaw groups with both home and expert groups. Each expert group is assigned one of the scenarios and brainstorms five potential barriers, writing these in the middle column. These expert groups then write an if–then statement for one of the barriers. Then, in their home groups, the

Example scenario	Lea had planned to exercise thirty minutes each day. Yesterday, she had planned to run two miles and then do twenty sit-ups. But her ankle didn't feel right yesterday. She thinks she twisted it a little that morning, and she wanted to give it a day to make sure it was okay. So instead of exercising yesterday, Lea decided to hang out with friends. Today, she was supposed to go swimming with a friend, but her friend had something come up and couldn't give Lea a ride to the pool. Lea decides that she'll just go home and relax and get back to her exercise plan tomorrow.
Barrier 1	She had two instances where she couldn't do the specific type of exercise that she had planned to do that day (when she couldn't run because she didn't want to hurt her ankle and when she couldn't swim because she didn't have a ride to the pool).
Strategy	Have backup plans with other exercises to do already in mind for each day. For instance, if she couldn't run, then she could still do the sit-ups she had planned, along with yoga or another low-impact exercise that wouldn't have affected her ankle. When she couldn't swim, maybe she could do the running that she didn't do the day before.
Barrier 2	She had other options for spending her time that maybe seemed more fun than exercising (hanging out with friends and going home to relax).
Strategy	Practice positive self-talk and visualize positive results to convince herself to stick to her schedule when she is tempted to do something else.
Scenario 1	Darius has been having trouble getting to school on time. He made a plan to set his alarm ten minutes earlier than he used to and move the alarm clock across the room so that he has to get up to turn it off. This worked when he first tried it at the beginning of the week, but now Darius has been late again three days in a row. Even worse, he stayed up late last night finishing his homework, but he couldn't find it this morning when he gathered his materials for the day, so he's going to get marked down for a late assignment, in addition to being marked tardy.
Barrier 1	
Strategy	
Barrier 2	
Strategy	
Additional ideas from group	
Scenario 2	For English class, Marisol is working on a research paper where each student chooses a topic and has one month to complete the paper. When she received the assignment, Marisol made a plan with the steps of finding sources, completing her research, and writing the paper. She worked backward from the final due date to assign deadlines to each of the smaller steps, and by the end of the first two weeks, she should have chosen sources and done half of her research. But now it's Friday on the second week, and Marisol just settled on a topic last night. Now she only has two weeks left, and she hasn't even started on the first step of her plan—finding sources. Even worse, she was just assigned a project in her biology class, and she doesn't know how she'll be able to complete the work for both classes and turn in quality finished products.
Barrier 1	
Strategy	
Barrier 2	
Strategy	
Additional ideas from group	

FIGURE 4.4: BARRIERS AND STRATEGIES.

*Visit **go.SolutionTree.com/SEL** for a free reproducible version of this figure.*

Scenario	Five Potential Barriers (What could get in my way?)	If–Then Statements to Address Two of the Barriers
Example: You have trouble remembering to finish your mathematics assignments, so you decide to spend thirty minutes right after school completing the daily assignment before you do anything else (homework or fun).	1. My friends are doing something after school that I really want to do. 2. I get distracted and spend twenty of my thirty minutes on my phone. 3. I don't understand the concepts in the homework and don't know how to finish it. 4. I'm tired; I think I'll do the mathematics homework later. 5. I forgot about an after-school event (such as a sibling's game) that will last a few hours and that I can't miss.	1. *If* I don't understand the homework, *then* I will call a friend who does well in mathematics to ask for help. 2. *If* I am too tired or unfocused to do my mathematics homework right away, *then* I will choose a specific new time that evening to do it and set an alarm so I don't forget.
1. You often eat sugary foods during the day and experience a sugar crash every afternoon. You plan to eat healthier foods so that you will feel more alert in the afternoon.		
2. Your school requires volunteer hours. The counseling office has a list of opportunities, but you're not sure where you want to volunteer and are feeling nervous about calling places to ask about volunteering.		
3. You have a big test in two weeks. You plan to study each evening.		
4. You want to save $100 to go to a concert with your friend in four months.		
5. It seems like your room is always messy, and you want to change that. You decide to spend fifteen minutes each evening tidying it up so that it will stay clean.		
6. When working on your chemistry assignment, you often get frustrated and give up. You decide that you'll count to ten, and then use your notes to figure out the problem that you got stuck on.		

FIGURE 4.5: WRITING IF–THEN STATEMENTS.

*Visit **go.SolutionTree.com/SEL** for a free reproducible version of this figure.*

expert for each scenario describes the barriers and their if–then statement. The home groups write if–then statements to address two additional obstacles for each scenario.

Wrap up the activity by asking each group to share one unique if–then statement. Remind students that managing distractions or other barriers could include things like changing how you approach something (such as setting alarms for your study breaks so that you aren't tempted to take longer breaks than needed) or changing your environment (for example, you might start studying on your own at home if you end up doing more talking than studying when you study with friends after school). When we are able to anticipate barriers, we can determine how we will avoid or overcome them before they even happen.

WHAT TEACHERS SAY

"Students used self-regulation to complete a semester-long Genius Hour project. As we continued to develop the competency, the students were more in tune with the changes they needed to make to get their project done and were more self-reflective about the process."

—Rikki, history teacher

Activity 49: Making Choices That Work for You

Individually, have students read the scenarios in figure 4.6 (page 90), determine what they would do next in that situation, and consider what the likely outcome of their decision would be (columns 2 and 3 in the table). Then, in groups, have students discuss their responses and determine alternate choices and the associated outcome they would expect. This activity is intended to help students strengthen their ability to consider how various actions and decisions affect outcomes. Remind students that there are numerous options for how we could choose to react in any given situation, and there usually isn't a right or wrong option. Explain to students that numerous options always exist, but sometimes we limit ourselves to all-or-nothing thinking— either doing something perfectly or not doing it at all. When answering, they should consider how they personally would be likely to respond in the situation; their answer might be complex or partially dependent on other factors. Explain that self-regulation isn't just about always making what you think is the responsible choice, it's about thinking through which actions and strategies will be most effective in helping you reach your goal while still being realistic about the other demands on your time, attention, and energy.

Review the completed example in figure 4.6 (page 90) with students. In this example, it's not about just saying that you would skip the activity with your friends so that you can stick to your goal; it's about being realistic about what the result of each choice might actually look like, and making sure that you're not ignoring the fact that sometimes you need to take a break and have fun in order to be able to be productive when working toward your goals.

Wrap up by asking students if they were able to identify multiple options for each scenario. Ask for volunteers to share examples from their own lives of times when they were able to balance fun activities while still staying on track to reach their goals.

Scenario	What would you do?	What's the likely outcome of your choice?	What other choice or choices could you have made? What would be the likely outcome then?
Example: You made a plan to improve your English grade (read twenty pages of your novel each night to finish two weeks before the report is due and write a quality report). You had the flu for three days and didn't do any reading. You had planned to catch up by reading thirty pages for each of the next three days. But you just heard that tomorrow your friends are going to dinner at your favorite restaurant and to a movie you're dying to see, and you know that if you join them, you won't have time to do your planned reading.	I really want to join my friends tomorrow, especially since I've spent the last few days being miserable with the flu. But I also want to make progress on my reading so that I can still meet my deadline for finishing the book. To do both, I will plan to read forty-five pages tonight, join my friends for dinner and a movie tomorrow, and read another forty-five pages the next day.	I will be able to hang out with my friends while still meeting my goal. I will also have a chance tomorrow to monitor my progress (did I get the forty-five pages read tonight?) and update my plan based on that information.	I could have chosen to stick to my plan and not go with my friends, which probably would have gotten me back on track. But I also would have felt disappointed and frustrated about missing out, which would make it harder to focus on reading. I could have chosen to go with my friends and keep my plan to read thirty pages tonight and the day after tomorrow, just skipping tomorrow's reading. This would have let me hang out with my friends but wouldn't have gotten me back on track for my reading goal.
1. You want to reduce your gaming time from four hours a night to two hours, so you have more time for things like doing your homework, seeing friends, and helping around the house. You made a plan and stuck to it for two weeks, spending ninety minutes or fewer gaming each day. Today, you have plans with a friend after school, and you have chores to do tonight. A game you're really excited about was just released and your sibling just bought it and asked if you want to go home to play it now. You know if you start, you won't stop for hours.			

2. You're on the basketball team; your free throw success rate is 25 percent in games this year. You want to get to at least 75 percent, so you made a plan to practice free throws on your own for thirty minutes every day after team practice. After two weeks, you're at 60 percent in your individual practice. However, you still only made 25 percent in last night's game. After the game, a few teammates gave you a hard time about how much you've practiced without making any difference in your game performance.			
3. You've been sent to the office twice this month for disrupting class. You sit by a friend, and sometimes when you're both finished with your work and waiting for the next task, you start talking and don't realize you're being disruptive until it's too late. You made a plan to focus on other things (reading ahead on the next topic for that class, doing homework for other classes, listing that day's homework and when you will complete it) to help you keep from being disruptive with your friend. It worked yesterday, but today your friend wants to show you something on his phone and is hurt when you say no.			

FIGURE 4.6: DETERMINING OUTCOMES FROM CHOICES.

*Visit **go.SolutionTree.com/SEL** for a free reproducible version of this figure.*

Activity 50: Situational Judgment Assessment

Ask students to independently read the scenario and answer the prompt. This scenario extends through each chapter, building on prior answers. A reproducible form with all situational judgment assessments is provided in appendix A (page 153).

SCENARIO

In health class, Alex and his classmates learned about the benefits of drinking an adequate amount of water each day. Alex has decided that he does not drink enough water.

Write three if–then statements that address obstacles Alex is likely to encounter.

Review each student's answer to determine whether the if–then statements address barriers that would likely impact Alex's water consumption. Examples might include the following.

- If I forget my water at home, then I'll buy one from the vending machine.

- If I haven't drunk enough water before lunch, then I'll finish what's in my water bottle before I start eating.

- If I don't like the taste of the water at school, then I'll keep liquid flavoring in my backpack.

Independent Practice With Feedback

Through independent practice, students begin applying their learning to their own endeavors. This promotes fluency of the skills and provides opportunities for formative feedback and coaching. Your goal is for students to evaluate their monitoring efforts to determine if their plans are off track, identify any obstacles that are derailing them, determine specific actions and strategies to get back on track, and incorporate the new actions into their future monitoring efforts.

WHAT TEACHERS SAY

"I asked students, 'What worked? Were you successful?' And if you're not, it's not a huge ordeal. We can go back and make those changes at any point. The important part to understand is that if it's not working, that's the time to learn."

—Jill, chemistry teacher

Activity 51: Addressing Distractions Within Your Self-Regulation Efforts

Have students take a few minutes to review the plan that they created in activity 24 (page 49) or activity 25 (page 51). Then have students individually fill out figure 4.7 by writing at least five distractions or challenges they've encountered (or are likely to encounter), listing three ways to manage or resist the distraction or challenge, and writing an if–then statement for one of the potential solutions. Encourage students to make their potential solutions and if–then statements as realistic as possible, considering what they would actually do to effectively address the challenge. This activity can be completed in partners or groups if students are having difficulty determining multiple options for managing distractions and challenges.

Distraction or Challenge	Three Possible Ways to Manage or Resist This Distraction or Challenge	One If–Then Statement for Managing the Distraction or Challenge
Example: Even though I set aside 3:30–4:30 to work on homework, I typically end up spending at least fifteen minutes (and sometimes thirty minutes) of that time on my phone.	1. Schedule a phone break from 4:00–4:10 and set alarms so I stick to that schedule. 2. Put phone in airplane mode for the hour. 3. Use wall clock to track time; put phone in another room or ask someone to hold it for me.	*If* I am tempted to check my phone during my homework hour, *then* I will ask my mom to hold my phone until my homework is done.
1.	1. 2. 3.	
2.	1. 2. 3.	
3.	1. 2. 3.	
4.	1. 2. 3.	
5.	1. 2. 3.	

FIGURE 4.7: MANAGING DISTRACTIONS IN YOUR SHORT-TERM PLAN.

Visit go.SolutionTree.com/SEL for a free reproducible version of this figure.

Facilitate a class discussion during which each student shares one if–then statement. Provide encouragement and strategic feedback as needed.

Activity 52: Contingency Planning for Academic Success

Explain that we are going to use mental contrasting to motivate us to do well in school by following the steps outlined in figure 4.2 (page 84). Tell students that, for step 1, their goal is to do well in school. Have them imagine the benefits of doing well in school. Then prompt students to think about obstacles related to specific classes and assignments and visualize themselves overcoming these hurdles.

After the mental contrasting exercise, ask students to write down a few of the hurdles that they are likely to encounter in the next couple weeks and then write if–then statements to address each obstacle. Remind students that we need to balance our time with activities that we consider work and play. Writing if–then statements helps us think through options that balance progress toward our goals with other demands on our time. Encourage students to share their if–then statements with a partner who can ask about their progress or provide reminders if a barrier is encountered.

Review students' contingency plans. Look for commonalities among the students and consider providing discussion time for students to continue to brainstorm together and share their successes. Follow up by prompting students to add their contingencies to their monitoring processes and future self-regulation plans.

Summary

We all encounter obstacles—they can't be avoided. However, by thinking about the barriers in advance, we can design strategies for addressing these challenges before they happen. The reproducible instructional planning tool (page 96) provides a guide for planning your instruction. By practicing self-regulation, we take responsibility for our own success, shifting our thoughts from blaming external influences to empowering ourselves to enact strategies for overcoming the obstacles. Students often give up when they encounter challenges, but by normalizing the barriers (understanding that we all encounter them), we can guide students to focus on solutions that work for them. Persevering through obstacles leads to greater self-efficacy, thereby creating a positive cycle and promoting more success.

Determine whether you will customize the vignettes or adapt activities to resonate with your students. Then consider how you could provide ongoing practice and feedback to students. Select instructional activities that will help your students meet the initial instruction, guided collaborative learning, and independent practice learning targets.

Adjusting Your Plan

INSTRUCTIONAL PLANNING TOOL

Initial Instruction: Students acknowledge that everyone faces obstacles and that it is possible to overcome those obstacles by adjusting their efforts.	
Instructional Activities	Notes and Adaptations
Activity 41: Reflecting on Past Obstacles Activity 42: Famous People on Overcoming Obstacles Activity 43: Is Your Phone a Tool or Distraction? Activity 44: Mental Contrasting Activity 45: Check for Understanding	
Guided Collaborative Learning: Students anticipate common obstacles and determine adjustments for specific situations.	
Instructional Activities	Notes and Adaptations
Activity 46: Anthony Gets Off Track While Saving Money Activity 47: Connecting Barriers and Strategies Activity 48: Writing If–Then Statements Activity 49: Making Choices That Work for You Activity 50: Situational Judgment Assessment	
Independent Practice With Feedback: Students evaluate their monitoring efforts to determine if their plans are off track and identify the obstacles that are derailing them, then determine specific actions and strategies to get back on track and incorporate the new actions into their future monitoring efforts.	
Instructional Activities	Notes and Adaptations
Activity 51: Addressing Distractions Within Your Self-Regulation Efforts Activity 52: Contingency Planning for Academic Success	
How will you provide ongoing practice addressing each learning target?	
When and how can you provide feedback to each student?	

CHAPTER 5

REFLECTING ON YOUR EFFORTS AND OUTCOMES

Reflection is an internal process of consciously looking back at experiences, drawing conclusions, and applying that information to future planning. Through reflection, we ponder, clarify, and self-appraise to deepen our self-awareness and determine optimal next steps. We analyze our strengths and areas for growth and take actions to improve. While we've listed reflection as the fourth self-regulation component, it occurs throughout the self-regulation process as we plan, monitor, and adjust our actions to meet a goal. The self-evaluation aspect of reflection promotes the continued use of self-regulation strategies and increases our self-efficacy by connecting our actions with the corresponding results or progress (Cleary & Zimmerman, 2012; Scholer, Ozaki, & Higgins, 2014). Reflection can be particularly helpful when encountering challenging or difficult situations, as it helps us find meaning, learn about ourselves, and make connections.

WHAT TEACHERS SAY

"The reflection piece really helped them to feel confident that through self-evaluation and reevaluation, they can make changes and SEE positive effects—they were really thinking about how they think, learn, and behave."

—Kimberly, English language arts teacher

Reflection on outcomes is important, but the process of self-evaluating the underlying efforts that led to an outcome is even more important. For example, students often wait to receive a grade on a test to determine whether they are doing well in class—in fact, many students do not make the connection between a test grade and their learning (or the effort they put into learning and preparing for the test). To help students understand the relationships between actions, learning, and grades, teachers may add reflection questions to tests.

- How prepared do you feel to take this test?

- What steps did you take to learn the material and prepare for the test?

- How well do you understand the content being assessed? What percentage of the content of this test have you mastered?

These questions focus the students' reflection on their *learning* rather than on their *grade*, promoting an emphasis on students' mastery of the skill or concept rather than simply on their performance. The most successful students self-evaluate their own learning (Frey et al., 2018) and take ownership of learning by reflecting on their preparation, content mastery, and performance together rather than in isolation.

Let us again revisit the students in Mrs. Cooper's class and their research project.

Mrs. Cooper's Research Project

Students are getting ready to turn in their research projects. As they worked in class this past week, Mrs. Cooper prompted students to provide constructive feedback to each other and use the rubric to self-assess their performance. Students then revised their writing based on peer feedback and self-appraisal. Mrs. Cooper has continued to have students meet in their monitoring groups as well as have individual conferences with her. She knows that nearly every student is on track for meeting the deadline, and the few students who are behind have reasonable plans for catching up and finishing on time. The buzz in the classroom is positive. Clearly students feel good about their progress toward completing their papers.

Students have been monitoring, reflecting, and adjusting throughout the process, but Mrs. Cooper realizes that this is an important moment to reflect on their self-regulation efforts overall and determine habits they want to maintain going forward. Pointing to the self-regulation poster hanging in her classroom, she asks students what it means to reflect. Great points are made by students, and she moves to the next question, "What specifically should we reflect on related to the process of writing our best-ever research papers?" Students share numerous important considerations including reflecting on the monitoring techniques, the effectiveness of their initial plans, the adjustments they made along the way, their learning and performance, strategies that helped them stay motivated, and time-management techniques. Mrs. Cooper next asks students how they might reflect. As with the monitoring techniques, there is variation, with some students wanting to think quietly and write while other students want to share through conversations with classmates. Both seem like viable options, so Mrs. Cooper provides class time for students to discuss or write their reflections.

When students turn in their research papers a few days later, Mrs. Cooper takes the reflection a little further by asking students to write letters to their future selves. She reminds students that they will be writing another research paper next semester, so in this letter they are going to remind themselves of actions, behaviors, and strategies that helped them produce quality research papers. At the end of each letter, Mrs. Cooper prompts the students to add a postscript describing at least one element of the research paper that was their personal best. In doing this, she is guiding students to reflect on their learning. Mrs. Cooper collects and reads each letter, internally celebrating each student's success. She plans to hand these letters out when she introduces the next writing project in a couple months.

Teachers can help students reflect by providing practice opportunities and process-oriented feedback. Students will gain a better understanding of how they learn by monitoring their development of skills, evaluating the effectiveness of their specific learning and study techniques, and more closely examining how gains in learning are directly associated with the effort they expended (Zimmerman, 2013). Reflection is also a key aspect of changing behaviors and attitudes, helping us build better relationships and handle interpersonal challenges. The instructional activities in this chapter are designed to increase students' ability to reflect on the effectiveness of their planning, monitoring, and adjusting; reflect on the resulting outcomes; and then apply this knowledge to future endeavors.

Outline of Instructional Activities

- **Initial Instruction:** Your goal is for students to be able to articulate the purpose of reflection, methods for reflecting, and how reflection promotes self-regulation.

  - ➤ **Activity 53**—Why Should We Reflect?
  - ➤ **Activity 54**—Running Without Looking at Progress
  - ➤ **Activity 55**—Thinking About Our Thinking
  - ➤ **Activity 56**—Reflection Techniques
  - ➤ **Activity 57**—Check for Understanding

- **Guided Collaborative Learning:** Your goal is for students to be able to determine reflection methods and outcomes for a variety of situations.

  - **Activity 58**—Ava Reflects on Her Energy
  - **Activity 59**—Reflecting on Levi's Public Speaking
  - **Activity 60**—Preparing for a Capstone Project
  - **Activity 61**—Situational Judgment Assessment

- **Independent Practice With Feedback:** Your goal is for students to engage in self-directed reflection throughout the self-regulation process.

  - **Activity 62**—A Letter to Your Future Self
  - **Activity 63**—Reflecting on Learning
  - **Activity 64**—Your Roadmap to Success

Initial Instruction

Through these activities, students learn critical self-regulation concepts, make connections to their lives, and build a shared vocabulary. Your goal is for students to be able to articulate the purpose of reflection, methods for reflecting, and how reflection promotes self-regulation.

Activity 53: Why Should We Reflect?

Refer to the self-regulation poster (figure 1.2, page 20), and briefly remind students of the four self-regulation components: plan, monitor, adjust, and reflect. Applying a think-pair-share strategy, ask students to think about what it means to reflect, briefly discuss with a partner, and then share their thoughts with the class. As students share, jot down synonyms and key phrases. Use this information to develop a class-identified definition of reflection. Your class definition might resemble this definition of reflection: reflection is an internal process of consciously looking back at experiences, drawing conclusions, and applying that information.

Explain to students that reflection is a vital part of self-regulation because, if we don't consider where we struggled and what helped us succeed, we won't learn as much as we could from the experience. In other words, whether or not we accomplish our goals, without reflection we will not gain the important deeper understanding of ourselves, including of our abilities and areas for growth, our best methods for personally mastering challenging skills or tasks, and of how we can continue to grow and improve.

Activity 54: Running Without Looking at Progress

Share this analogy with students: working through a self-regulation plan without taking time to reflect during and after your efforts is like competing in the 400-meter race in track without ever reviewing your times or thinking about your progress. Prompt students to share their thoughts on this analogy.

Continue the conversation by asking students how reflecting is related to the other components of self-regulation—planning, monitoring, and adjusting. In the analogy, the athlete should be monitoring both progress in running faster and the actions that led to this progress. Then the runner can reflect on whether the workouts are effective and whether he or she put enough effort into achieving a better time. The runner might also reflect on adjustments that he or she has made or could make in the future. Overall, this reflection would help to refine the plan going forward.

Conclude the discussion by explaining that you wouldn't run track without looking at your times or thinking about the exercises that have helped you get faster, so you shouldn't work on a self-regulation plan without reflecting on what you can learn from it and how you can use that knowledge going forward. Reflecting will not only support your analysis of progress toward your goals but also improve your future efforts as you identify the specific components of self-regulation that you struggle with most, the strategies that were most effective for you, and ways that you might want to change or refine your approach in the future.

WHAT STUDENTS SAY

"My reflection process happens as I monitor my progress. I look at my checklist to see how I'm coming with my plan. If I'm off track, I reflect on what I did wrong. After completing a goal or task, I not only reflect on whether I got it done on time, but also on my moods throughout. I think about if I was stressed or anxious and what can I do next time to relieve that."

—Tenth-grade student

Activity 55: Thinking About Our Thinking

Now that students have learned about and begun practicing self-regulation, explain that they are learning metacognitive skills; in other words, they are thinking about their thinking. Using the following questions, ask students to reflect and self-judge their learning by giving a thumbs up for "yes," a thumbs down for "no," or pointing their thumb sideways if they are somewhere in between.

- Can you explain what it means to self-regulate?

- Can you describe the difference between monitoring progress and monitoring actions?
- Can you write an if–then statement for a specific distraction?

Ask students to partner up to discuss the activities that helped them learn self-regulation—was it something in the class discussions, the scenarios about different students, or having to develop their own self-regulation plans? Then have partners share one answer with the class. Ask the class if they need you to give them a test or a grade in order to know whether they have learned more about self-regulation. The answer should be "no." Explain that students never need to wait for a grade to reflect on their learning or how they feel about a test. Wrap up the conversation by explaining that they just reflected on their learning and the types of activities that most effectively support their learning. This is important for all of us to do regularly.

WHAT TEACHERS SAY

"I think our kids are so busy that they might not get a chance to really sit back and think about how they can improve on something. They know that they're not the best at something, but giving them the time and space to really think about how they can improve on that is huge. . . . The benefits I saw with using this were that the kids got the time and space and the guidance to create a plan and to reflect on that as well."

—Caitlin, technology teacher

Activity 56: Reflection Techniques

Remind students that reflection is an internal process of consciously looking back at experiences, drawing conclusions, and applying that information to future planning. Through reflection, we ponder, clarify, and self-appraise to deepen our self-awareness and determine optimal next steps. We analyze our strengths and areas for growth, and then we take actions to improve. Explain to students that there are many strategies and tools that we can use to support our reflection efforts. Ask students to share ways they might reflect. Options may include journaling, keeping a video log, talking with a friend or parent, and just thinking.

Prompt students to individually list questions that they could ask themselves to promote their reflection throughout the self-regulation process. Using a cooperative learning strategy such as speed dating, have students pair up for one minute with the goal of sharing a question that the other person hasn't listed. The student then adds this question to his or her list. Students rotate to different partners and repeat the task. This continues for up to ten rotations.

Now that every student has a long list of questions, ask them to categorize each question under the component where they think it best fits (planning, monitoring, adjusting) or at the conclusion of a project or goal. An example is provided in figure 5.1.

Reflection Questions

- Reflection while planning:
  - Is my plan likely to lead to my goal?
  - Do I have enough details in my plan?
  - Am I committed to following my plan?
- Reflection while monitoring:
  - Am I monitoring all the aspects of my plan?
  - Am I monitoring my progress toward my goal?
  - Am I monitoring often enough?
  - Are my monitoring techniques working for me?
- Reflection while adjusting:
  - Am I making progress and staying on track with my plan?
  - What adjustments will work best for me?
  - What strategies are most effective for managing distractions?
  - How effective are the adjustments I've made?
  - How have I overcome challenges?
- Reflection at the conclusion:
  - Did I follow my plan and complete all the steps?
  - Was I successful in accomplishing my goal or mastering a skill? If I wasn't successful, did I still make progress?
  - Were the things I decided to monitor actually helpful in promoting my progress?
  - Was I able to identify things that weren't working and address them in time to get back on course?
  - What parts of my plan worked the best?
  - What do I want to improve for next time?

FIGURE 5.1: REFLECTION QUESTIONS.

Visit go.SolutionTree.com/SEL for a free reproducible version of this figure.

Wrap up the activity by explaining that reflection not only helps us identify things that are meaningful and important, but it also helps highlight things that aren't important or are ineffective so that we can eliminate unnecessary steps and play to our strengths. We can also identify things that would have made the tasks easier or better. You likely know the saying hindsight is 20/20, which refers to the fact that it is easier to see why something went wrong after it has already happened. But we can learn from hindsight by reflecting on our mistakes and our successes and applying what we have learned to our future efforts.

Activity 57: Check for Understanding

Using response cards or an online quiz platform, gather individual students' responses to the items displayed in figure 5.2. Review the responses to ensure that students understand how reflection supports self-regulation. Reteach as necessary. [The answer key for figure 5.2 is: 1–d; 2–c; 3–false; 4–false; 5–true.]

---

1. When should you reflect?

    a. After I have reached my goal

    b. When I am monitoring and adjusting my plan

    c. As I make my plan

    d. All of the above

2. Which of the following best describes the purpose of reflection?

    a. Pointing out everything I've done wrong

    b. Focusing only on my strengths so that I can build on them

    c. Self-evaluating what works well for me and determining changes to my efforts for future planning

    d. Identifying what could go wrong so that I can avoid it

True or False

3. _____ When reflecting, it is important to compare my performance to others so that I know I am working hard enough.

4. _____ Reflection is most important after I have reached a goal. It's not necessary if I give up on my goal.

5. _____ I don't need a test grade to reflect on my preparation for a test.

FIGURE 5.2: CHECK FOR UNDERSTANDING—REFLECTING.

*Visit **go.SolutionTree.com/SEL** for a free reproducible version of this figure.*

Guided Collaborative Learning

Scenario-based activities address an array of circumstances to which adolescents can relate. Through these collaborative-learning activities, students gain a deeper understanding of self-regulation concepts. Your goal is for students to be able to determine reflection methods and outcomes for a variety of applicable situations.

Activity 58: Ava Reflects on Her Energy

In activity 19 (page 42), we learned that Ava followed a plan to increase her energy. Using the same scenario (reprinted following this paragraph and reproducible from appendix C, page 163), guide students through a discussion of how Ava analyzed her actions along the way to achieve her goal. The scenario doesn't use the word *reflect*, but Ava clearly gave healthy eating some serious thought. Prompt students with the questions, "What does Ava notice about herself? What does she think about?" Reading one sentence at a time, ask students to annotate by making thought bubbles for Ava. For example, after reading the first sentence, students may make thought bubbles that say, "I don't have any energy" or "I wish I didn't spend so much money on junk food."

SCENARIO

Ava lacks energy and spends too much money on energy drinks and cookies (her daily lunch). She falls asleep every afternoon in algebra and doesn't feel well in general. She wants to eat healthier, so she decides to change her diet to low-sugar, minimally processed food and shift to eating more protein, fruits, and vegetables. She gives away all her energy drinks and writes out a menu of what she will eat for breakfast, lunch, dinner, and snacks (using a nutritional guidance website to make sure that her menus will help her meet her goals). She discusses the plan with her family and asks her mom to stop buying cookies. She then records her food intake using an app. She gets off track at a weekend party, eating chips and cookies. The next day, she decides to keep granola bars and dried fruit in her purse so that she has an alternative to chips and cookies when at parties. Each day she reviews the data in the app, tracking nutrients consumed in relationship to recommended daily allowances, and she thinks about whether she ate a balanced diet that followed her menu. Using a printed calendar, Ava then gives herself one to five stars for her effort that day and writes one personal success or challenge she experienced. Weekly, she thinks about what is working and what isn't, and then she revises her plan accordingly. She now has much more energy, stays awake in algebra, and feels healthier overall.

Wrap up the activity by asking students when Ava reflected. Ensure that students understand that Ava reflected before making a plan, while planning, and while implementing her plan. When self-regulating, we too should reflect throughout the process.

Activity 59: Reflecting on Levi's Public Speaking

Let's return to Levi's scenario, where he is feeling anxious about public speaking (activity 22, page 46, and activity 36, page 67). Don't worry if you didn't use the prior activities; the scenario that follows provides all the information needed for this activity. This scenario is reproducible from appendix C (page 163). In small groups, ask students to discuss the question at the end of the scenario. Encourage students to be specific and come up with at least five questions that Levi could ask himself. For example, "Did taking deep breaths help me feel calmer?" might be a question Levi could ask himself.

SCENARIO

Your friend Levi is taking a public speaking class. He knows that he will be expected to speak in front of groups in the career he plans to pursue. The only problem is that Levi gets very anxious when speaking in front of a group. His palms sweat and his mouth gets very dry. He ends up talking too fast and without emotion. Levi made a plan for feeling confident and reducing his anxiety when giving a speech. He followed this plan, which included practicing the speech many times in front of family, taking deep breaths before each practice speech, pausing in the middle to remember to speak slowly and with emotion, and repeating the phrase, "I am prepared for the speech. I can do this!" Yesterday, Levi gave his speech. Since it is a public speaking class, another speech has already been assigned. What should Levi think about when making his plan to master his next speech?

Pair up the small groups to share the questions that they developed and further discuss the scenario. Wrap up the activity by asking students to reflect on anxiety-reducing strategies they have tried. Discuss ideas for ways to reduce anxiety.

Activity 60: Preparing for a Capstone Project

If your school requires a capstone, Genius Hour, or senior project, use the details of the project for this activity. If a long-term project isn't a requirement for graduation at your school, use the following scenario, reproducible from appendix C (page 163). Ask students to form groups based on the subject they would likely focus on for their project (mathematics and science, engineering, language arts, art and music, and so on) and then determine how they would reflect in preparation for the capstone project. What past experiences would they think about? What questions would they ask themselves? How would this information influence their self-regulation plan for completing the project?

> **SCENARIO**
>
> To graduate, you must successfully complete a capstone project that demonstrates your knowledge and skill. It is expected that the project will take about six months for you to complete and will include research, a portfolio outlining your process, and a final product that demonstrates your achievement. How might you reflect on your strengths and past challenges as you prepare to take on this project?

Ask groups to briefly share with the class. Provide specific praise and feedback to each group. Wrap up the discussion by asking if they think reflecting in the beginning would help them be more successful in completing the capstone project.

Activity 61: Situational Judgment Assessment

Ask students to independently read the scenario and answer the prompt. This scenario extends through each chapter, building on prior answers. A reproducible form with all situational judgment assessments is provided in appendix A (page 153).

> **SCENARIO**
>
> In health class, Alex and his classmates learned about the benefits of drinking an adequate amount of water each day. Alex has decided that he does not drink enough water.

Write three questions that Alex could use to guide his reflection. Identify when and how Alex will reflect on his progress and actions.

Review each student's answers to determine whether the reflection occurs at frequent intervals and goes beyond monitoring. Example questions might include the following.

- How is my water consumption impacting the way I feel?
- On days when I drink enough water, what am I doing to be successful at this?
- On days when I don't drink enough water, what am I missing or forgetting to do?
- Overall, is my health improving by increasing my water consumption?

Alex could reflect daily using a log.

Independent Practice With Feedback

Through independent practice, students begin applying their learning to their own endeavors. This promotes fluency of the skills and provides opportunities for formative feedback and coaching. Your goal through these instructional activities is for students to engage in self-directed reflection throughout the self-regulation process.

Activity 62: A Letter to Your Future Self

Have each student identify an accomplishment or difficult task that he or she has achieved. If students are having trouble coming up with ideas, you might help them brainstorm by sharing the following examples.

- Working hard on a project and learning the content
- Practicing skills to improve performance in a sport or artistic endeavor
- Researching or watching a video on how to do something and then following the directions to accomplish the task
- Replacing a bicycle or car part by thinking it through and following directions

Prompt students to write letters or create videos that they can use to encourage themselves when they encounter challenges. In this letter, they should describe the situation, reflect on the challenges they encountered, and identify how they overcame these challenges. They should also describe how it felt to meet the goal and encourage themselves so that they can accomplish other challenging goals.

Wrap up by reminding students that this activity is really about self-reflection. It is taking a moment to think about what they did to achieve, grow, or learn. Before starting a complex assignment or project, consider having students read their letters to focus on growth mindset in preparation for the challenge.

WHAT TEACHERS SAY

"There are more conversations about what students need to do for themselves and how it's not up to me to be making sure they're doing all these things, but it's up to them to not only do them but to go back and reflect on what they're doing."

—*Janelle, algebra 1 and 2 teacher*

Activity 63: Reflecting on Learning

When giving a test, prompt students to reflect by adding these questions to the test (the first two at the beginning and the third question at the end).

1. How prepared do you feel to take this test?

2. What steps did you take to learn the material and prepare for the test?

3. How well do you understand the content being assessed? What percentage of the content of this test do you think you have mastered?

These questions focus the students' attention on their learning.

Then, when you hand back the graded test, prompt students to review their answers to the reflection questions, their performance, and your feedback, and then answer these three reflection questions.

1. What? Report the facts objectively. (Student summarizes how he or she performed on the test.)

2. So what? Analyze the information. (Student carefully considers and summarizes his or her reflection question answers, test performance, and teacher feedback.)

3. Now what? Consider future options. (Student describes key takeaways or thoughts and how he or she can apply them to future tests.)

These questions prompt students to review their efforts and teacher-provided feedback rather than just focus on their grade. Prompting this reflection on a regular basis helps students analyze the relationships between actions, learning, and performance.

Activity 64: Your Roadmap to Success

Ask students to think about their self-regulation efforts related to an academic or personal goal (such as their self-regulation plans from activity 24, page 49, or activity 25, page 51). Prompt students to draw a map that illustrates their step-by-step path toward their goal while also including roadblocks and detours they encountered along the way. Encourage students to include details about the adjustments that have helped them move toward their goal.

Once students have drawn their maps, have students work in small groups to describe their paths to improvement on a specific goal. Prompt the groups to provide encouragement and offer additional details they could add to the map. Review each student's illustrated map and provide specific feedback, including improvements you have seen the student make and questions the student might consider going forward (for example, Have you thought about . . . ?). Extend the activity by prompting students to review and add to their maps at regular intervals.

Summary

While it can be challenging for us, reflection is a key component of self-regulation that occurs before, during, and after our efforts to meet a goal. The reproducible instructional planning tool provides a guide for planning your instruction. If we fail to reflect, we miss important insight and understanding, which allow us to more efficiently and effectively complete activities and accomplish tasks toward a goal. Like the other components of self-regulation, reflection is a set of skills that we can learn and practice through scenarios, situations, and application in our own lives. In doing so, we improve our understanding of ourselves and are better able to take on the challenging tasks ahead.

Determine whether you will customize the vignettes or adapt activities to resonate with your students. Then consider how you could provide ongoing practice and feedback to students. Select instructional activities that will help your students meet the initial instruction, guided collaborative learning, and independent practice learning targets.

Reflecting on Your Efforts and Outcomes

INSTRUCTIONAL PLANNING TOOL

Initial Instruction: Students articulate the purpose of reflection, methods for reflecting, and how reflection promotes self-regulation.	
Instructional Activities	Notes and Adaptations
Activity 53: Why Should We Reflect? Activity 54: Running Without Looking at Progress Activity 55: Thinking About Our Thinking Activity 56: Reflection Techniques Activity 57: Check for Understanding	
Guided Collaborative Learning: Students determine reflection methods and outcomes for a variety of applicable situations.	
Instructional Activities	Notes and Adaptations
Activity 58: Ava Reflects on Her Energy Activity 59: Reflecting on Levi's Public Speaking Activity 60: Preparing for a Capstone Project Activity 61: Situational Judgment Assessment	
Independent Practice With Feedback: Students engage in self-directed reflection throughout the self-regulation process.	
Instructional Activities	Notes and Adaptations
Activity 62: A Letter to Your Future Self Activity 63: Reflecting on Learning Activity 64: Your Roadmap to Success	
How will you provide ongoing practice addressing each learning target?	
When and how can you provide feedback to each student?	

CHAPTER 6

PUTTING IT ALL TOGETHER

As we describe in chapter 1 (page 13), self-regulation is a complex internal process associated with metacognition, motivation, behavior, and the management of emotional reactions. In order to effectively self-regulate, we must plan, monitor, adjust, and reflect. If we plan without monitoring, we won't know whether we are making progress. If we skip reflection, we don't improve our self-awareness and aren't able to apply this knowledge of ourselves to future efforts. Together, the four components of self-regulation create a fluid, cyclical, self-improvement process that propels us to progress through planned tasks and behaviors to reach goals. Through self-regulation, students become more self-aware, increase their self-efficacy, and apply skills that enable them to persevere in reaching their goals (Schunk & Greene, 2018; White & DiBenedetto, 2018).

WHAT TEACHERS SAY

"Now that we have taught self-regulation, students are more apt to set goals, follow steps, and realign their plans in order to achieve their goals."

—David, principal

While students may understand and use self-regulation processes in a particular setting, this does not necessarily mean that they will generalize the competency by applying self-regulation strategies effectively across all contexts. Deliberate practice with ongoing feedback in diverse situations promotes students' understanding and application of self-regulation concepts. We can compare our instructional path up to this point to driver's education:

students understand the rules of the road and can likely pass the written test, but they still need the opportunity to apply their knowledge in practical settings to become fully proficient drivers. Similarly, as students regularly practice using self-regulation to achieve many different goals, they will build the experience needed to become competent and capable of applying these skills across academic, social, and personal endeavors.

Let's return once again to Mrs. Cooper's class.

Mrs. Cooper's Research Project

We adjusted the story of Mrs. Cooper's English class interspersed throughout the previous chapters (with her permission) to streamline the narrative and emphasize key instructional practices. In reality, in her classroom, Mrs. Cooper began the year teaching students how to both summarize research articles and use self-regulation strategies within the context of writing research summaries. She scaffolded the learning by co-constructing the self-regulation plan as a class for the first article synopsis and then expanding students' responsibility for two more article synopses prior to starting the research paper. As we describe in prior chapters, Mrs. Cooper then facilitated students' practice of self-regulation while they worked on their research papers. She found that not only did students embrace the added responsibility, but they also increased their academic performance through each iteration of planning, monitoring, adjusting, and reflecting. In reflecting on the impact of self-regulation instruction, Mrs. Cooper noted that students' papers were of higher quality than in past years (based on the grading rubric), and their general homework completion and grades improved. Out of 150 students, only five missed the research paper deadline, a much-improved statistic over prior years.

Think about teaching self-regulation the same way you would think about coaching a high school soccer team. Students may move up from the junior varsity to the varsity team, but that doesn't mean they no longer need coaching. In fact, the amount of practice time often increases after people master fundamental skills. Similar to coaching, your grading practices and feedback influence the use of self-regulation strategies (Cleary & Chen, 2009; Hadwin, Jarvela, & Miller, 2018; Harks, Rakoczy, Hattie, Besser, & Klieme, 2014). In reviewing our self-regulation instruction up to this point, we see that students are now able to demonstrate the components of self-regulation. Next, they need to combine the skills and concepts to improve their fluency in self-regulating across various environments. The instructional activities in this chapter are designed to increase students' ability to analyze efforts to self-regulate, determine opportunities to apply their self-regulation knowledge, and design self-regulation plans that promote ownership over learning.

Outline of Instructional Activities

- **Initial Instruction:** Your goal is for students to articulate the self-regulation components and determine how self-regulation is beneficial now and in the future.
  - ➤ **Activity 65**—Self-Regulation Components
  - ➤ **Activity 66**—Benefits of Self-Regulation
  - ➤ **Activity 67**—Check for Understanding
- **Guided Collaborative Learning:** Your goal is for students to analyze situations and determine how each component of self-regulation could be improved.
  - ➤ **Activity 68**—Finding Missing Components in Academic Self-Regulation
  - ➤ **Activity 69**—The Impact of Missing Components on Ava's Energy
  - ➤ **Activity 70**—Elijah Studies for an Exam
  - ➤ **Activity 71**—Teaching Others
  - ➤ **Activity 72**—Situational Judgment Assessment
- **Independent Practice With Feedback:** Your goal is for students to analyze their self-regulation habits and knowledge and then apply the self-regulation process to their own endeavors.
  - ➤ **Activity 73**—Assessing Your Self-Regulation Again
  - ➤ **Activity 74**—Analyzing Results
  - ➤ **Activity 75**—Planning for Success

Initial Instruction

Through these activities, students learn critical self-regulation concepts, make connections to their lives, and build a shared vocabulary. Your goal is for students to articulate the self-regulation components and determine how self-regulation is beneficial now and in the future.

Activity 65: Self-Regulation Components

If you have the self-regulation poster (figure 1.2, page 20) displayed in your classroom, cover it up for this activity. Ask students if they can name the four components of self-regulation without looking at a visual reminder or asking a friend. Have students hold up fingers representing the number of components they can name. Then, call on a student to share one component, continuing until students have named all four components.

Next, ask each student to think about why the self-regulation planning component is important and what might happen if it is missing from their efforts to self-regulate. Follow the think–pair–share format to provide time for each student to formulate his or her own reasons and share them with a peer. Ask for volunteers or call on groups to share with the class. Repeat the think–pair–share process for each of the other components (monitoring, adjusting, and reflecting). Conclude the activity by emphasizing that all four components of self-regulation are necessary, and if we skip a component, we likely won't be as successful in whatever we are working to achieve (Noonan & Gaumer Erickson, 2018).

Activity 66: Benefits of Self-Regulation

Remind students that the ability to self-regulate will be important throughout their lives, not just in school. Ask them to brainstorm some ways in which adults they know try to self-regulate. Provide additional examples as necessary (such as getting to work on time, exercising, healthy eating, managing time, saving money, and using a calm voice when frustrated), emphasizing that self-regulation is critical to success not only in school but also in adult life.

Figure 6.1 lists some specific abilities that are supported by self-regulation— as we improve our self-regulation skills, we also improve our ability to develop and maintain these specific behaviors (Gaumer Erickson & Noonan, 2019). As a class, discuss how the abilities listed relate to self-regulation, adding these ideas to the middle column. Prompt each student to fill out the third column independently, thinking about how each listed ability is or will be important for him or her.

Then have students complete the last four rows in figure 6.1 by working individually to identify additional abilities or behaviors that self-regulation will help them develop. If students are having difficulty coming up with additional ideas, you might suggest the ability to stick to a budget, identify and apply for specific opportunities such as jobs or scholarships, balance work and social life, or improve in a sport. Encourage students to share their ideas with each other.

WHAT TEACHERS SAY

"A lot of our students were struggling to complete the tasks that they were assigned to do outside of class or outside of their internship experience because they weren't planning ahead. This was a great teaching tool for me to show these kids why self-regulation would be important throughout the semester and how they could better use some of these tools in order to help meet their goals . . . . Students are now using the self-regulation learning from their internship class and applying it to some of their other classes."

—*Greg, high school internship coordinator*

Ability to:	How is this ability related to self-regulation?	Why is this ability important for me now and in adult life?
1. Control my temper (self-regulate my anger responses)		
2. Maintain healthy behaviors (like eating mostly healthy foods or going to bed at a reasonable time)		
3. Plan and work through a long-term project		
4. Be on time		
5. Meet a deadline		
6. Learn a skill		
7.		
8.		
9.		
10.		

FIGURE 6.1: BENEFITS OF SELF-REGULATION.

*Visit **go.SolutionTree.com/SEL** for a free reproducible version of this figure.*

Activity 67: Check for Understanding

Using response cards or an online quiz platform, have students individually identify the component for each behavior displayed in figure 6.2 (page 118). Review the responses to ensure that students understand the components of self-regulation. Reteach as necessary. [The answer key for figure 6.2 is: 1–adjust; 2–monitor; 3–reflect; 4–plan; 5–reflect.]

Identify which self-regulation component each behavior addresses.	
Behavior	**Component**
1. Changing your study methods after you realize that just reading the chapter summary isn't helping you learn	Plan Monitor Adjust Reflect
2. Telling a friend about your progress each day	Plan Monitor Adjust Reflect
3. Thinking about successes, setbacks, and specific things you have learned	Plan Monitor Adjust Reflect
4. Working backward from the due date to create a timeline	Plan Monitor Adjust Reflect
5. Considering your past efforts when setting new goals (such as what you did well and what you could change)	Plan Monitor Adjust Reflect

FIGURE 6.2: CHECK FOR UNDERSTANDING—SELF-REGULATION COMPONENTS.

Visit **go.SolutionTree.com/SEL** for a free reproducible version of this figure.

Guided Collaborative Learning

Scenario-based activities address an array of circumstances to which adolescents can relate. Through these collaborative-learning activities, students gain a deeper understanding of self-regulation concepts. Your goal is for students to analyze situations and determine how each component of self-regulation could be improved.

Activity 68: Finding Missing Components in Academic Self-Regulation

Together, review the example scenario in figure 6.3. Describe how each component was rated on a scale from 1 (weak) to 5 (strong) with an explanation of each rating and one idea for improvement. Then, working in small groups, have students read the scenario in figure 6.4, discuss and rate how well each of the four self-regulation components is addressed, and briefly explain the rating. Next, have students brainstorm strategies for improving each component.

Don't worry about whether there is some variation in students' ratings for each component, so long as they can justify their ratings. In Mia's scenario, her plan may be adequate for completing missing assignments, but she doesn't include test preparation in her self-regulation efforts. Even if a student rates a component of self-regulation as strong, he or she should be able to determine ways to improve that component.

Activity 69: The Impact of Missing Components on Ava's Energy

Let's return to the scenario in which Ava wants to increase her energy. It's fine if you didn't complete activity 19 (page 42) or activity 58 (page 104); the scenario provides all of the information you need for this activity and is

Example scenario: Jayden was given an assignment to write an essay in three weeks. The last time he had an assignment like this, he didn't write the paper until the night before it was due, and he didn't get a good grade. To do better this time, he makes a self-regulation plan. Per Jayden, "I will break the assignment down into the basic parts (choose a topic, outline the essay, write the supporting paragraphs, write the introduction and conclusion, make revisions as necessary, and write the final draft), estimate how much time each part will take, and then work backward to identify deadlines for completing each part. After finishing the essay, I'll reflect on the quality of my work."

	Plan	Monitor	Adjust	Reflect
Rate how well each component is addressed in the scenario. (1 = weak, 5 = strong)	3	1	1	2
Brief explanation for your rating	It includes the start of a plan (identifying steps for completing the project and setting deadlines for each), but it is not a full plan for accomplishing the steps.	Jayden's plan doesn't include any ideas for monitoring his progress or actions.	Jayden is missing potential challenges or ideas for adjusting as needed.	Jayden only reflects at the end about the final product.
One idea to make each component stronger	Schedule time to work on the essay.	Monitor twice a week by checking each task off and listing strategies to stay focused.	Think about challenges and write if–then statements (such as *if* I have trouble choosing a topic, *then* I will ask my teacher for guidance).	During and after the assignment, regularly reflect on progress, strategies that are working, and what's not working.

FIGURE 6.3: FINDING MISSING COMPONENTS—EXAMPLE SCENARIO.

*Visit **go.SolutionTree.com/SEL** for a free reproducible version of this figure.*

Scenario: Mia really wants to improve her grade in American history. Per Mia, "I need to improve my grade in American history. Here is my plan: I'll figure out if I have any missing assignments, turn in missing assignments, and then get a good grade on next Monday's test." Mia wrote down all her missing assignments and then crossed each assignment off the list after she completed it. On the following Tuesday, Mia reflected that she turned in her missing assignments, but she received a poor grade on Monday's test. She isn't sure where she went wrong.

	Plan	Monitor	Adjust	Reflect
Rate how well each component is addressed in the scenario. (1 = weak, 5 = strong)				
Brief explanation for your rating				
One idea to make each component stronger				

FIGURE 6.4: FINDING MISSING COMPONENTS.

*Visit **go.SolutionTree.com/SEL** for a free reproducible version of this figure.*

reproducible from appendix C (page 163). Using the jigsaw strategy, assign four students to each home group. Share the scenario with students and explain that this scenario includes all four components of self-regulation. Assign each expert group one of the four components of self-regulation (plan, monitor, adjust, or reflect). These expert groups discuss what might have happened if Ava had not addressed the assigned component of self-regulation. Then, in their home groups, the expert for each component describes the impact of missing that component, and the home groups discuss the importance of including all four components within efforts to self-regulate.

SCENARIO

Ava lacks energy and spends too much money on energy drinks and cookies (her daily lunch). She falls asleep every afternoon in algebra and doesn't feel well in general. She wants to eat healthier, so she decides to change her diet to low sugar, minimally processed food and shift to eating more protein, fruits, and vegetables. She gives away all her energy drinks and writes out a menu of what she will eat for breakfast, lunch, dinner, and snacks (using a nutritional guidance website to make sure that her menus will help her meet her goals). She discusses the plan with her family and asks her mom to stop buying cookies. She then records her food intake using an app. She gets off track at a weekend party, eating chips and cookies. The next day, she decides to keep granola bars and dried fruit in her purse so that she has an alternative to chips and cookies when at parties. Each day she reviews the data in the app, tracking nutrients consumed in relation to recommended daily allowances, and thinks about whether she ate a balanced diet that followed her menu. Using a printed calendar, Ava then gives herself one to five stars for her effort that day and writes one personal success or challenge she experienced. Weekly, she thinks about what is working and what isn't, and then she revises her plan accordingly. She now has much more energy, stays awake in algebra, and feels healthier overall.

Activity 70: Elijah Studies for an Exam

The following scenario provides a detailed plan for preparing for a final exam. This scenario is reproducible from appendix C (page 163). In groups, prompt students to discuss Elijah's scenario, list how he addresses each self-regulation component, and brainstorm ways his plan could be improved.

SCENARIO

Elijah wants to get a B on his biology final. Per Elijah, "I'll create a study schedule, I'll complete two sections of the study guide each night, and I'll finish the study guide in five days. While I fill out the study guide, I'll make flash cards for any vocabulary terms that I don't already know. Next, I'll review all my previous tests from the semester and correct the answers I got wrong. I'll also quiz myself on all the vocabulary terms. Finally, I'll review all the diagrams for each concept, and I'll write down any questions I have and ask my friend Liam, who is amazing at biology, to explain anything I don't understand. I've got a plan, so I think I'll do well on the final." After two days, Elijah reviewed his plan and checked on how he was doing: "Well, I only got one section of the study guide done, and I didn't write any vocabulary cards (because I don't have any index cards) for the section I did. I need to make some changes. I'll buy a pack of index cards from the school store before I go home today. I'll review the section that I did do for any vocabulary terms. I'll create flash cards for those terms. Next, to get caught up, I'll do all of sections 2 and 3 tonight and half of section 4. Tomorrow, I'll finish section 4 and do sections 5 and 6. I'll also make sure I keep up with the vocab flash cards. Then I'll be back on track."

Debrief as a large group by talking through the group's responses to the scenario. Wrap up by again emphasizing the importance of using all four components to self-regulate successfully.

WHAT TEACHERS SAY

"I found that, for the most part, students had better self-esteem because they felt they had more control over their learning environment. They were able to make a plan and reflect on the plan and obtain higher grades and more control of their lives."

—Nicholas, special education teacher

Activity 71: Teaching Others

The purpose of this activity is for students to teach self-regulation to other students by creating videos. Explain that these videos might be used to teach students in future classes about self-regulation. Encourage students to work in groups and be creative—the videos can be live action, animation, or voice over. Each video must include a scenario that applies all four components of self-regulation.

Visit **go.SolutionTree.com/SEL** for a link to an example of a student video. In this video, Izzy describes self-regulation and applies the components to improving in basketball.

> *Izzy's script: Self-regulation is a proactive, self-directed process for attaining goals, learning skills, managing emotional reactions, and accomplishing tasks. Being proactive means planning ahead of time, not last minute. Self-directed means on your own; nobody is making you do something. Process means actions put together over time to make progress toward a goal. This is where you actually achieve your goal and what you have been working toward.*
>
> *Self-regulation can be used in all areas of life including school, sports, jobs, chores, and emotions. For example, if you are a basketball player and were only able to make 25 percent of the free throws in the last game, self-regulation could help you get better. You could plan practice time just for free throws and monitor the amount of time you actually practiced and your free-throw percentage (how many you can shoot out of ten) at the end of each practice. If you're not improving as quickly as you hoped, adjust your plan by getting advice from teammates or coaches on your form. Reflect on your efforts to improve your free-throw percentage and your performance in games. (Research Collaboration, 2020)*

Prior to producing the videos, have students review each other's outlines or scripts and provide feedback that includes both praise and suggestions. When providing feedback, students should consider the following three questions.

1. Is the situation realistic (could it really happen)?

2. Does it address all four components of self-regulation?

   ➤ Planning

   ➤ Monitoring

   ➤ Adjusting

   ➤ Reflecting

3. Is it interesting and could other students learn from it?

After the students complete the video productions, watch the videos as a class. Consider spreading them out over time as a review activity in which students watch and discuss one video per class session.

Activity 72: Situational Judgment Assessment

Ask students to independently read the scenario and answer the prompt. This scenario extends through each chapter, building on prior answers. A reproducible form with all situational judgment assessments is provided in appendix A (page 153).

Review the plan that you developed for Alex to drink more water. Now that you know more about the importance of all four self-regulation components, what would you add to his plan?

Analyze each student's response looking for detailed description for improving planning, monitoring, adjusting, and reflecting. Provide specific, constructive feedback to each student.

Independent Practice With Feedback

Through independent practice, students begin applying their learning to their own endeavors. This promotes fluency of the skills and provides opportunities for formative feedback and coaching. Your goal is for students to analyze their self-regulation habits and knowledge, and then apply the self-regulation process to their own endeavors.

Activity 73: Assessing Your Self-Regulation Again

Now that students have learned about self-regulation, ask them to complete the Self-Regulation Questionnaire and Knowledge Test again (provided in appendix B, page 157). While you can copy the assessment and have students complete it on paper, it functions more effectively when students complete it digitally. To administer online, log back into your free account on researchcollaborationsurveys.org. Follow the directions on the website to launch the Self-Regulation Questionnaire and Knowledge Test. Through this site, students will receive a summary of their results immediately after completing the assessment, and as the teacher, you will be able to access composite class results, individual summaries, and a complete data file.

If you are administering the Self-Regulation Questionnaire and Knowledge Test through the researchcollaborationsurveys.org website, provide students with the survey link and code. If possible, provide the link digitally to save time. Remind students to enter their student-specific number (school ID), or you can assign each student a number. This will allow you, as the teacher, to review their individual results. Be sure to remind students that after finishing the test, they should stay on the results page for the next part of this activity.

Tell students that, for items 1–28, as they read each item, they should pause for a moment to think about the last few weeks and how well they were able to self-regulate in various situations. For instance, they might consider how often they submitted course assignments on time or how well they accomplished personal goals like saving money, improving in a sport, or learning a new skill. Explain that items 29–49 test knowledge of self-regulation concepts and potential ways to effectively self-regulate in certain situations. The test results will help them better understand how they currently self-regulate and measure their knowledge of self-regulation concepts. Give students adequate time to complete the assessment (ten to fifteen minutes).

After students submit the test, a results page automatically displays. Using these results, ask each student to complete figure 6.5. The self-assessment scores are displayed on a 100-point scale, so they can be interpreted as percentages (similar to the interpretation of grades). The knowledge score is displayed as a total out of 20 items. Students can calculate their percentage correct by dividing the number of correct answers by 20 and multiplying by 100.

Review each student's summarized results and provide feedback and encouragement. Use the teacher view on the website to access both individual and aggregate student results. Log back into your account on http://researchcollaborationsurveys.org, scroll to the list of *My Surveys*, locate your survey, and click on the *View* button to open the teacher view for that survey. You'll see an aggregate graph of students' scores on each component and overall, followed by a breakdown of student responses to the self-reflection items. Then you'll see the percentage of students who answered each knowledge item correctly followed by the class average. Review these results and determine concepts to reteach.

Please note that the Self-Regulation Questionnaire and Knowledge Test is a formative assessment designed to guide instruction and promote student reflection. Analyze the results along with data from other valid sources to determine whether a student may benefit from further instruction or targeted practice.

WHAT STUDENTS SAY

"I just completed the posttest and earned 100 percent. I clearly know a lot more about self-regulation than when I started these activities. My self-assessment graph shows that I am now demonstrating self-regulation consistently in my life. I believe self-regulation is a skill that would benefit all teenagers as well as adults."

—Eleventh-grade student

Component	Self-assessed score (from graph)	Rank order components from 1 (highest) to 4 (lowest); if two components have the same score, choose the one that you feel is higher	One item for each component that depicts your strengths	One item for each component that depicts your areas for improvement
Making plans				
Monitoring plans				
Adjusting plans				
Reflecting on what works and what to improve				

	Score	Calculated percentage	One item answered correctly	One item answered incorrectly
My self-regulation knowledge score	____ /20			

FIGURE 6.5: MY SELF-REGULATION POSTTEST RESULTS.

Visit go.SolutionTree.com/SEL for a free reproducible version of this figure.

Activity 74: Analyzing Results

It is beneficial for students to compare their pretest and posttest data to reflect on their learning (pretest scores were documented in figure 1.6, page 26). Explain that student self-assessed ratings on each component may be lower now than on the pretest. This may be because students have learned more about themselves and about self-regulation, so now they are able to more accurately and critically judge their performance (Winne, 2018). The knowledge score (out of twenty) provides an indication of learning while the self-assessed component scores provide the students' perspectives on their own current behaviors.

Using their answers in figure 6.5 (page 125), ask students to reflect on their Self-Regulation Questionnaire and Knowledge Test results by responding to three questions either in writing or in a video recording.

1. What? Report the facts objectively on how you scored on both the pretest and posttest. Describe concepts that you didn't understand previously but do understand now.

2. So what? Analyze your test results and summarize what it means for you as a student (your educational pursuits) and an individual (your social and work pursuits).

3. Now what? Consider future options. How will you use what you have learned about the four self-regulation components in the next year? Five years?

Review students' responses and provide specific praise to each student, highlighting observed accomplishments or growth in self-regulation.

WHAT TEACHERS SAY

"Students have realized how much more they are able to complete and how much they have control over. Students were a lot more invested in the project than previous ones that I have given. They also were more serious about working as a team."

—Shelly, language arts teacher

Activity 75: Planning for Success

Now it is time for students to put all their learning together to develop and enact their own self-regulation plans. As described at the beginning of the chapter, students will need to practice within numerous contexts and a variety of goals. As the teacher, you can guide students to use self-regulation strategies to achieve many different outcomes (such as for projects, test preparation, and daily academic behaviors). You can also use your community of learners to support each other in self-regulating personal, social, extracurricular, or employment pursuits.

Once they have identified the goal or outcome, prompt students to develop their own self-regulation planning template that incorporates all four self-regulation components (an example template is provided in appendix D, page 171). Provide the reflection questions from activity 56, figure 5.1 (page 103) to guide students' planning. Encourage students to brainstorm together, share their plans, and provide feedback to each other (prompts are provided in activity 24, figure 2.8, page 50). As students enact their plans, provide regular prompts for them to monitor and reflect, brainstorm solutions to distractions and obstacles, and determine adjustments. Provide feedback and encouragement to each student regularly throughout their efforts to self-regulate.

Continue using your course content and school experiences to give students opportunities to practice self-regulation and take increasing responsibility for their own learning and effort. Use data from the posttest and performance-based assessments (see chapter 7, figure 7.2, page 134, and figure 7.3, page 135) to monitor students' growth and determine concepts to reteach. When students are struggling to self-regulate, ask questions that guide their thinking, encourage continued collaborative brainstorming, and remind them that everyone makes mistakes and has setbacks—that is why *adjusting* is a component of self-regulation.

Summary

Our efforts to teach students to self-regulate don't stop here. We are all continuing to practice self-regulation by planning, monitoring, adjusting, and reflecting. The reproducible instructional planning tool (page 128) provides a guide for planning your instruction. We should continue to coach and prompt students to self-regulate, but we no longer need to regulate for them. Our students are ready to take on the responsibility of self-regulating through continued deliberate practice, building their capacity to become socially and emotionally engaged, career equipped, lifelong learners.

Determine whether you will customize the vignettes or adapt activities to resonate with your students. Then consider how you could provide ongoing practice and feedback to students. Select instructional activities that will help your students meet the initial instruction, guided collaborative learning, and independent practice learning targets.

Putting It All Together

INSTRUCTIONAL PLANNING TOOL

Initial Instruction: Students articulate the self-regulation components and determine how self-regulation is beneficial now and in the future.

Instructional Activities	Notes and Adaptations
Activity 65: Self-Regulation Components	
Activity 66: Benefits of Self-Regulation	
Activity 67: Check for Understanding	

Guided Collaborative Learning: Students analyze situations and determine how each component of self-regulation could be improved.

Instructional Activities	Notes and Adaptations
Activity 68: Finding Missing Components in Academic Self-Regulation	
Activity 69: The Impact of Missing Components on Ava's Energy	
Activity 70: Elijah Studies for an Exam	
Activity 71: Teaching Others	
Activity 72: Situational Judgment Assessment	

Independent Practice With Feedback: Students analyze their self-regulation habits and knowledge, and then they apply the self-regulation process to their own endeavors.

Instructional Activities	Notes and Adaptations
Activity 73: Assessing Your Self-Regulation Again	
Activity 74: Analyzing Results	
Activity 75: Planning for Success	

How will you provide ongoing practice addressing each learning target?

When and how can you provide feedback to each student?

CHAPTER 7

MEASURING GROWTH IN SELF-REGULATION

Pause for a moment and reflect. Why are you teaching students to better self-regulate? What benefits and outcomes do you expect to see as a result of your instructional efforts? Our overarching goal is that adolescents generalize and apply self-regulation skills to their current and future lives, across education, employment, and community living settings. To achieve this objective, we need to confirm that students are learning the concepts and moving along the continuum of independence to becoming competent. To be competent, a person must proficiently acquire and perform the set of skills, as well as determine when and how to apply and customize self-regulation skills across environments and pursuits. As educators, we provide progressively challenging practice to foster independent and transferable application (see figure 7.1).

Source: © 2017 by Amy Gaumer Erickson and Patricia Noonan. Used with permission.

FIGURE 7.1: PROGRESSION TO COMPETENCE.

Individuals who demonstrate competence in self-regulation perform better in academic, employment, and social endeavors. In school, students who self-regulate earn better grades and higher scores on standardized assessments

(Frey et al., 2018; Hattie & Zierer, 2018; Zimmerman & Kitsantas, 2014). These students regulate their emotional reactions (Ivcevic & Brackett, 2014) and take ownership over their learning (White & DiBenedetto, 2018). When students learn how to evaluate the effectiveness of self-regulation strategies, they also improve their ability to accurately attribute their success to the effort they put in, creating a positive cycle that increases their confidence in their own abilities (Scholer et al., 2014; Zimmerman, 2013). To achieve these outcomes, students must first acquire the skills, then develop fluency, and finally generalize the skillset.

Assessment Techniques

There are numerous ways to measure students' abilities to self-regulate, many of which have been integrated into instructional activities in chapters 1 through 6. In this chapter, we will outline an array of assessment techniques that guide instruction and gauge students' self-regulation abilities across time and settings. We have organized this chapter around five sections, each addressing the assessment of progressively deeper self-regulation concepts. The corresponding five questions focus our formative assessment techniques on perceptions, knowledge, skills, application, and outcomes.

1. **Assessing perceptions:** Are students increasing their self-awareness and accurately analyzing their own self-regulation?

2. **Assessing knowledge:** Are students increasing their knowledge of self-regulation concepts?

3. **Assessing skills:** Are students increasing their skills in the four self-regulation components (planning, monitoring, adjusting, and reflecting)?

4. **Assessing application of skills:** Are students self-regulating across environments and endeavors?

5. **Assessing outcomes:** As students develop self-regulation, are academic, behavioral, and social outcomes improving?

Assessing Perceptions

Are students increasing their self-awareness and accurately analyzing their own self-regulation? To answer this question, we must consider input from students. The Self-Regulation Questionnaire, described in activities 10 (page 25) and 73 (page 123) and shown in appendix B (page 157), prompts students to reflect on behaviors associated with self-regulating in learning environments. The data from the twenty-eight self-report items, rated on a scale from *Not Like Me* to *Very Like Me*, promote students' appraisal of their relative strengths and areas for growth related to the self-regulation components. By reflecting on their composite ratings for items addressing the four components of self-regulation, as well as individual item ratings, students become more self-aware and are more likely to take action to increase their abilities.

Novice learners are often overconfident in knowledge and skills (Winne, 2018). After students have thoroughly learned self-regulation, they are better able to critically appraise their behaviors. Therefore, when the Self-Regulation Questionnaire is administered at the beginning and end of the instructional activities outlined in this book, the expectation is not that the students' ratings improve. Instead, the purpose of the Self-Regulation Questionnaire in activity 10 (page 25) is to prompt students to think about behaviors associated with self-regulation and to analyze their self-reported data to determine their relative strengths and areas for focused improvement in self-regulation. In activity 73 (page 123), the purpose is similar, but with greater awareness, the results can also inform ongoing purposeful practice and feedback.

The Self-Regulation Questionnaire can be administered prior to providing instruction and after students have learned the self-regulation components. It can also be used to refocus students' attention on self-regulation a couple times per year or when circumstances change (such as when transitioning between learning modalities). Students should evaluate their self-ratings to better understand their strengths in self-regulation and to determine specific areas for learning and improvement.

To promote ongoing reflection, students can frequently self-assess using the effort and learning chart in figure 3.7 (page 71). The rubric-type descriptions will help students accurately self-appraise their behaviors associated with effort and learning in numerous classroom settings. Students can use this self-assessment as often as daily and analyze results across time to examine the relationship between effort and learning.

WHAT STUDENTS SAY

"Learning about self-regulation has helped me get my work done and know what I need to do better."

—Eighth-grade student

Assessing Knowledge

Are students increasing their knowledge of self-regulation concepts? The instructional activities include the Self-Regulation Knowledge Test, checks for understanding, and numerous classroom activities you can employ to gauge knowledge. These assessments give you the data to measure learning over time and pinpoint areas to review or reteach. Knowledge assessments also support the development of assessment-capable learners by providing students evidence of their learning (Frey et al., 2018).

The Self-Regulation Knowledge Test, described in activities 10 (page 25) and 73 (page 123) and displayed in appendix B (page 157), is a curriculum-based measure that assesses students' knowledge of self-regulation concepts and judgment of the most effective course of action when applying these concepts. The test includes multiple choice, yes or no, true or false, and short answer items. You can use the Knowledge Test as a pretest (see activity 10, page 25) and a posttest (see activity 73, page 123). A comparison of scores can provide an indicator of knowledge growth. Analysis of the results can also pinpoint areas of misunderstanding requiring additional instruction.

In addition to the Self-Regulation Knowledge Test, the checks for understanding within each chapter (activities 5, 18, 31, 45, 57, and 67) assess students' knowledge around critical concepts. These short, formative assessments prompt students to assess their learning of critical concepts. The results determine whether there is a need for additional instruction. Teachers can also assess students' knowledge throughout the activities as students engage in discussions and provide their rationale for responses. These informal techniques, allowing for immediate corrections or reteaching, are as valuable as the traditional multiple-choice assessments in determining students' mastery of the concepts.

WHAT TEACHERS SAY

"I have seen improvement in my students' self-regulation in terms of awareness of what needs to be done without being told. Another area that has improved is the way my students conduct themselves in a much calmer and more regulated way—impulsive behaviors were minimized."

—Nerissa, special education teacher

Assessing Skills

Are students increasing their skills in the four self-regulation components (planning, monitoring, adjusting, and reflecting)? In each chapter, we have provided guided collaborative learning activities that are designed to develop students' skills in each self-regulation component. The situational judgment assessment (see activities 9, 23, 37, 50, 61, and 72) is a multi-part evaluation that extends through each chapter. Appendix A (page 153) compiles all the situational judgment assessment activities. As implied by the term, situational judgment is an assessment technique that asks students to determine the best course of action for a specific situation. The scenario that we have provided focuses on drinking an adequate amount of water. Teachers can formulate additional situational judgment assessments by modifying the scenario and prompts.

In addition to the situational judgment assessment, the collaborative learning and independent practice activities in each chapter provide evidence of skill development. Students' skills can be informally assessed through many of the collaborative activities; however, it can be difficult to evaluate the skills of individual students when they are working in groups. Many of the independent practice activities extend and personalize students' learning by asking them to apply the skills to their own priorities. Together these activities provide indicators of students' skills, and methods for assessing them in a variety of authentic settings over time.

WHAT TEACHERS SAY

"I had them set goals for themselves, then made check points to regularly monitor and reflect on their progress with a novel project they were assigned. They had eight weeks to read a novel from my reading list and write an essay. In the years past, a large number of kids would put it off until the end and then scramble to get it done, and it was usually of lower quality than they were capable of. After introducing self-regulation, I had more students reading regularly to meet the steps in their plans, more students turned in their papers early, and students earned higher grades than I saw in past years. I could tell that learning self-regulation made a difference in the way kids approached the project."

—January, English language arts teacher

Assessing Application of Skills

Are students self-regulating across environments and endeavors? The independent practice activities within each chapter guide students to begin applying their skills. Beyond the activities in the prior chapters, using the following reflection process empowers students to self-assess their self-regulation practice, while providing an opportunity for you to observe demonstrable behaviors associated with self-regulation.

The performance-based reflection in figure 7.2 (page 134) promotes students' reflection on their demonstration of self-regulatory behaviors within authentic situations. This four-item rubric guides students to determine the quality of their planning, monitoring, adjusting, and reflecting related to a specific task or project.

The performance-based observation in figure 7.3 (page 135) is designed to be embedded within authentic situations such as academic courses and extracurricular activities. Based on observations across time or in specific situations, rate each student's self-regulatory behaviors on the scale from *Beginning* to *Advanced*. The Self-Regulation Performance-Based Observation should be

Reflect on your self-regulation by rating your performance on a specific task or goal.

Task or goal: _____

Component	Limited Self-Regulation	Moderate Self-Regulation	Substantial or Thoughtful Self-Regulation
Planning	I didn't do much planning. I may have thought about it a little.	I thought about what I needed to do to accomplish this. I may have written down a little.	I planned this out with the details I needed to accomplish it. I thought about my past self-regulation efforts to make a plan that would work well for me.
Monitoring	I didn't do much to track my progress. I may have thought about it a little.	Occasionally, I thought about my progress in accomplishing the task and the effort I put into it. Other people may have reminded me to monitor my progress.	I monitored along the way, making sure I was on track to accomplish the task and thinking through the effort I put into it.
Adjusting	I didn't really adjust my plan, even when I should have.	I thought through some of the things that were getting in my way when I got off track.	I adjusted as needed to stay on track or modified my plan to accomplish this task. I thought about what was getting in my way when I got off track and made changes to address the issue.
Reflecting	I didn't reflect throughout the process. I may have reflected a little at the end.	Occasionally, I reflected on my effort and my progress. I may have reflected on my learning.	I reflected throughout the process on my effort, my progress, and my learning.

Source: © 2021 by Amy Gaumer Erickson and Patricia Noonan. Used with permission.

FIGURE 7.2: SELF-REGULATION PERFORMANCE-BASED REFLECTION.

*Visit **go.SolutionTree.com/SEL** for a free reproducible version of this figure.*

purposefully planned, as it is necessary to ensure students have opportunities to demonstrate the specific behaviors. For example, if the goal is for students to apply self-regulation to reading a novel, you could prompt students to plan, write if–then statements, monitor, and reflect. Then, you could evaluate students' demonstration of each self-regulation indicator. To display proficiency, students need to think critically about their strengths, areas for growth, and the task at hand in order to develop personalized approaches that capitalize on strengths and minimize potential obstacles.

Results from both the performance-based observation and reflection support students' personal evaluation of relative strengths and areas for improvement. Teachers can compare the self-ratings to observed behaviors, lending strength to the ratings or determining students' misperceptions regarding their knowledge or fluency. The results can also be used to reflect on whole-class instruction (including guided practice, coaching, and feedback) necessary for students to become proficient at the indicator. When reviewing the results for individual students, instructional support may be necessary to augment the learning and practice, focusing on growth toward proficiency in the indicators.

Based on observations across time or in specific situations, evaluate each student's performance.					
Beginning: Not yet able to demonstrate without scaffolding					
Emerging: Minimal or superficial demonstration; prompting likely required					
Proficient: Sufficient demonstration including self-appraisal and detailed, personalized application					
Advanced: Independent and consistent demonstration; teaches or prompts others					
Not observed is documented if there has not been the opportunity to observe the behavior performed by an individual student.					
Self-Regulation Sequence Indicators	**Beginning**	**Emerging**	**Proficient**	**Advanced**	**Not Observed**
Demonstrates the ability to create a plan to accomplish a task or set of tasks					
Identifies potential barriers to plan completion using if–then statements					
Monitors progress of efforts over time					
Plans and practices ignoring some distractions during a task, resulting in increased focus					
Reflects on strengths, challenges, effort, and outcomes related to self-regulation in specific situations					

Source: © 2021 by Amy Gaumer Erickson and Patricia Noonan. Used with permission.

FIGURE 7.3: SELF-REGULATION PERFORMANCE-BASED OBSERVATION.

*Visit **go.SolutionTree.com/SEL** for a free reproducible version of this figure.*

WHAT TEACHERS SAY

"Students' vocabulary and study skills improved. While the first was measurable by higher than average scores on tests, the second was monitored within class through reflection and discussion."

—*Michael, English language arts teacher*

Assessing Outcomes

As students develop self-regulation, are their academic, behavioral, and social outcomes improving? Schools collect numerous indicators of academic and social-emotional behaviors. A research-based outcome of learning self-regulation is that students improve their school performance, but to measure this impact, specific short-term and long-term indicators should be monitored. Schoolwide long-term indicators include grade point average, suspension and expulsion rates, graduation rates, and postschool outcomes. Short-term outcomes include attendance, reduction in tardiness, on-time assignment submission, and improved regulation of emotional reactions resulting in reduced office disciplinary referrals. Teachers can also monitor students' effective use of class time, quality of work, engagement in collaborative learning, and demonstration of learning through tests and projects.

As Peggy P. Chen and Héfer Bembenutty (2018) describe:

> Research with young children through adults has consistently demonstrated that learners who self-regulate by being proactive, selecting strategies, planning tasks, monitoring progress, adapting to changes, and sustaining efforts are more successful in their learning and academic performance than those who do not. (p. 407)

But as we have described throughout this book, to become competent in self-regulation, students may require numerous practice opportunities with ongoing feedback and reflection. Existing behavior management mechanisms, such as office disciplinary referrals, can be modified to become coaching conversations in which the student determines strategies and makes a plan to manage or avoid the situation that resulted in the referral. This approach adjusts the role of the administrator from disciplinarian to behavioral coach.

WHAT TEACHERS SAY

"What I noticed as an administrator was it gave me a language to talk to kids—a way to reinforce the information that they were learning."

—Sam, high school principal

Together, assessment data can inform instructional decisions. Furthermore, these data can guide students' ongoing reflection on their development of skills. To determine the positive impacts associated with self-regulation instruction, it is necessary to monitor the quality of instruction, students' learning and performance, and short-term outcomes. This chapter focuses on student assessment; the epilogue outlines implementation fidelity aspects that guide instruction.

WHAT TEACHERS SAY

"The high school taught self-regulation schoolwide and saw a 50 percent reduction in office disciplinary referrals and suspensions in one semester."

—Chris, superintendent

Assessment Considerations

The assessments outlined in this chapter were designed for middle and high school students (approximately grades 6 through 12). As you evaluate the usefulness of each assessment, consider your students' experiences, abstract reasoning, and reading comprehension. Provide accommodations when appropriate, such as reading the items aloud, explaining the items, or having a scribe fill in the response option. The items on the Self-Regulation Questionnaire and the Self-Regulation Knowledge Test are written at a sixth-grade reading level, per the Flesch-Kincaid readability score (Kincaid, Fishburne, Rogers, & Chissom, 1975).

Unlimited rights are given to educational professionals to administer the assessments and utilize the results for skill development and program improvement. Educators are expected to include the citation of the assessment within all dissemination of assessment items or results. The content of the assessments cannot be reproduced for research purposes or published in any profit-bearing format without prior written permission from the authors.

Measures of reliability and validity vary across assessment types. The measurement design and analyses were guided by the *Standards for Educational and Psychological Testing* (American Educational Research Association, American Psychological Association, & National Council on Measurement in Education, 2014). Technical specifications on the measures are available at www.researchcollaborationsurveys.org. The measurement design included literature reviews; analyses of existing self-regulation measures; and pilot testing, including interviews with educators, parents, and youth. These assessments were designed through ongoing collaboration among secondary educators and educational researchers with the intended purpose of providing formative data to guide instruction and promote students' self-appraisal and application of skills.

Construction of the measures began in 2013 with a thorough review of literature on self-regulation, including the related terms of self-management, goal-directed action, agency, executive functioning, self-determination, and time management. Abbreviated literature reviews, available in the form of elementary and secondary research guides, can be accessed at www.cccframe work.org. Existing measures were reviewed by a team of researchers. In collaboration with educators and youth, three educational professionals with doctorates in educational research and one licensed clinical social worker specializing in adolescent social-emotional development constructed the assessment items. This process promoted the content validity of the assessments.

Development included the analyses of measures of internal consistency including Cronbach's coefficient alpha, exploratory factor analyses, and correlations. As of December 2020, the Self-Regulation Questionnaire has been used as a self-reflection measure by more than 20,000 adolescents. The questionnaire was initially tested for internal consistency using Cronbach's coefficient alpha with 1,354 responses from middle school and high school students in 2015 (28 items; $\alpha = .889$). Exploratory factor analysis was performed to test the concept homogeneity, revealing that the questionnaire measured a single factor, referred to as self-regulation. Revisions were made to add clarity to items. In a sample of 3,599 adolescents who completed the questionnaire from October 2019 to December 2020, the Self-Regulation Questionnaire was found to be highly reliable ($\alpha = .896$), with internal consistency above $\alpha = .88$ and maintained for each grade level, 6–12, and gender subgroup. In this same sample, the Self-Regulation Knowledge Test demonstrated good reliability ($\alpha = .731$). These analyses provide evidence of the reliability of the measures (Gaumer Erickson et al., 2020).

Structural validity included factor analyses with scree plots to examine the correlations among items. Additionally, item analyses were conducted to determine the positive discrimination of each item (for example, do students who perform well on the assessment overall perform better on the item than students with lower full-scale assessment scores). In the December 2020 sample of 3,599 adolescents, all items on both the Self-Regulation Questionnaire and the Self-Regulation Knowledge Test were found to discriminate positively. In other words, students who performed better overall were more likely to provide the correct or more positive response for each item.

To evaluate fairness of the assessments, demographic data, including grade and gender, were collected as part of the questionnaire and knowledge tests. Overall, females reported higher self-regulatory behaviors than males. Females also scored higher on the knowledge assessment than males. Statistically significant, but not functionally significant, effect size differences were found across grade levels on the questionnaire, with high school seniors providing higher ratings than students at other grade levels. Pretest knowledge scores also improved slightly as students advanced in school, from a mean of 48.6 percent correct for sixth graders to 64.9 percent correct for twelfth graders. No significant differences were found among schools with high and low free and reduced lunch rates, diversity levels, or urbanicity classifications. Race, ethnicity, and poverty differences at the individual student level have not been tested as these demographics are not collected through the assessments.

Substantive validity considers the meaning of the assessment data. We conducted item testing with adolescents using a think-aloud format where the students verbalized their thought process while answering the items. These students also identified items that were confusing or may be interpreted by adolescents differently than by adults. Revisions were made to enhance response specificity and applicability to adolescents. Through a beta-testing process, teachers guided students through a reflection procedure on assessment results. The teachers then provided feedback to the researchers regarding students' depth of reflection and usefulness of the data attributed to the measurement. Educator focus groups were conducted to determine the perceived accuracy of results and how the results promoted students' application of skills. This action-oriented reflection is a primary purpose of the formative assessments.

Generalizability was evaluated in part through correlations between assessments. In a sample of 3,599 adolescents who completed both the questionnaire and knowledge test between October 2019 to December 2020, we established that the measures correlated positively (0.267), a finding significant at the .01 level. The Self-Regulation Questionnaire focuses on self-reported behaviors while the Self-Regulation Knowledge Test assesses knowledge of core concepts; it is expected that these measures correlate positively but not perfectly.

Consequential validity evaluation included regression analyses. When used as a predictive variable for quarter 1 grade point averages, the questionnaire, knowledge assessment, and gender were found together to predict 29.88 percent of the variance in the end-of-quarter grade point averages for these students (Gaumer Erickson et al., 2020). Grade point average and course performance are described in the research as key outcome variables associated with self-regulation (Frey et al., 2018; Zimmerman & Kitsantas, 2014).

WHAT TEACHERS SAY

"During student-led conferences, we started hearing the students telling their parents, 'Well, I made a plan to do this. It didn't quite work how I wanted it to, so these are the changes that I made and this is how I knew it wasn't working.' We were hearing them use that language throughout the whole school—it wasn't just my classes anymore. It was everybody! That was so awesome to hear."

—*Alix, special education teacher*

Data-Based Decision Making

We have mentioned that these assessments are formative. It's not the assessment itself that differentiates between formative and summative measurement; it is the way in which the assessment results are used. Prior to administering any assessment, you should answer these two questions: How will the results be used by students to promote their learning and application of skills? How will the results be used by educators and leadership in my school to guide instruction? When appropriate, this third question should also be considered: How will data be shared with the student's family to promote school–family partnerships? When combined with other data sources, these assessments guide decision making regarding direct instruction to build students' knowledge, guided practice to develop students' fluency, and independent practice with ongoing coaching to promote students' proficiency and generalization.

By determining the areas of the self-regulatory processes to pinpoint, teachers can enhance their instructional practices. After facilitating continual guided and independent practice with feedback, teachers can readminister the Self-Regulation Questionnaire and Knowledge Test and, based on the results, alter instructional plans to further bolster students' self-regulation knowledge and skills. Measures of applying self-regulation skills, such as the performance-based reflection or observation, can be incorporated into classroom procedures. These assessments promote students' ongoing self-appraisal and reflection and deepen application of the self-regulation components—planning, monitoring, adjusting, and reflecting.

Summary

Through self-regulation assessments, we can measure students' perceptions, knowledge, skills, application, and outcomes. The reproducible assessment planning tool provides a guide for assessment planning. These data then guide our instruction and enhance students' self-appraisal. As educators, we are well versed in determining whether students are learning the academic content, then reteaching when necessary to ensure students learn and meet standards. The same premise applies to teaching self-regulation—we provide quality instruction, facilitate practice with feedback, and continually confirm learning through formative measurement. By applying numerous assessment techniques, students and teachers can monitor the development of self-regulation skills, fluency, and generalization, and as students learn and develop self-regulation, see desired short-term and long-term academic, behavioral, and social outcomes.

Measuring Growth in Self-Regulation

ASSESSMENT PLANNING TOOL

Identify assessment techniques to incorporate into your context. Consider how the assessment data will be used to inform instruction and promote students' reflection.

Assessment Type	Assessment Techniques
Assessing perceptions Assessing knowledge Assessing skills Assessing application of skills Assessing outcomes	

When and how will assessment data be collected?

How will the data be used to guide instruction?

How will the data be used to promote students' reflection?

How will the data be shared with students' families to promote school–family partnerships?

NEXT STEPS

While many of our students come to us unable to adequately self-regulate, we can provide quality instruction grounded in research to build the skills that will promote students' success. Most students cannot develop self-regulation solely from watching adults model skills; instead, they must be explicitly taught and given opportunities to practice over time.

The activities in this book are designed to truly build adolescents' self-regulation skills so that these skills can be applied to current and future personal, academic, and professional endeavors. When we teach content, we don't just provide the information one time and expect students to understand completely. Instead, we scaffold instruction, help students relate to the content, and monitor their growth. The same is true for social-emotional learning. The six instructional criteria (Gaumer Erickson, Noonan, & Cooper, 2017) in figure E.1 (page 144) illustrate how quality instruction is directly tied to self-regulation skills becoming a generalizable and transferable competency. As shown in the diagram, initial instruction addresses the first three criteria: increasing students' motivation to learn by evaluating their strengths and challenges, determining how self-regulation applies to them personally, and increasing their comprehension of vocabulary associated with self-regulation. Then, in the guided practice stage of instruction, students begin to apply their learning. Ongoing feedback and student-centered reflection lead to independent practice and proficiency. As shown in the diagram, we continue to practice self-regulation throughout our lives, but as teachers, we have a limited window of time to provide instruction and offer feedback to develop and enhance the skills of our students.

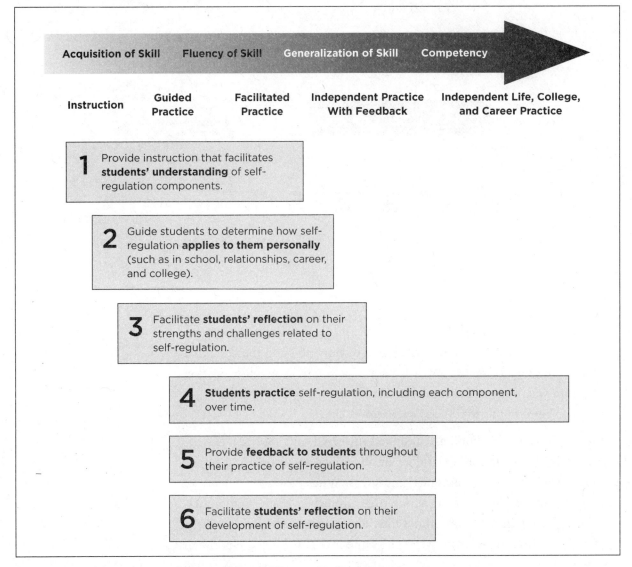

Source: © 2017 by Amy Gaumer Erickson and Patricia Noonan. Used with permission.

FIGURE E.1: INSTRUCTIONAL CRITERIA.

*Visit **go.SolutionTree.com/SEL** for a free reproducible version of this figure.*

Just like mastering challenging mathematics or language arts content, for students to develop strong self-regulation abilities, they need numerous instructional activities and practice opportunities across their school experiences. We can't just tell students what self-regulation is—we have to go deeper, including regularly revisiting the concept and promoting students' practice, ensuring that they not only fully understand the concept but also can effectively apply this knowledge. Social-emotional learning (SEL) research has shown that students are most likely to develop and generalize intrapersonal skills when they are given consistent opportunities to practice, with feedback, in authentic situations (Frey et al., 2018; Usher & Schunk, 2018; Yeager et al., 2018).

"One of the things that's important to remember is that we have to get past the 'Well, kids should already know how to do this by now' attitude. We have to be intentional about the way we go about providing self-regulation instruction. We can't just throw it out there and hope it sticks."

—*Sarah, language arts teacher*

Teacher Versus Student Roles

Often with the best intentions, teachers regulate for students, creating detailed plans *for* students and then monitoring their progress. We break assignments down into detailed tasks and timelines. We tell students the best study methods from our perspective. As we shift from regulating for students to them self-regulating, we still provide a high level of support for students, but in different ways. Figure E.2 (page 146) illustrates the teacher and student roles in self-regulation instruction. Initially, the teacher provides instruction around all four components (plan, monitor, adjust, and reflect) through a variety of instructional activities, including scenario-based applications. The role of the teacher then shifts as each student makes a plan, monitors it, adjusts, and reflects. While students practice the components, teachers continually provide coaching through feedback, prompting, listening, and questioning, but they do not provide directives (regulating for the student). Throughout, teachers assess and facilitate reflection to support students' understanding of their growth in developing self-regulation. In this way, we are not just helping students build a set of skills, but transferable competence that will allow them to determine when self-regulation is needed and apply the skills to a variety of situations.

Systematic Teacher Implementation

Implementing self-regulation instructional activities in your classroom is an excellent start toward helping students become competent self-regulators. As you begin implementing competency instruction, you may wonder if you are on the right track. Whether you are teaching virtually, face-to-face, or in a hybrid format, the Competency Framework Practice Profile for Teachers (Noonan, Gaumer Erickson, Heger, & Loewenstein, 2020) in figure E.3 (page 147) helps educators determine the degree to which they are addressing key indicators of implementation on a scale of *Novice, Emerging,* and *Proficient.* The practice profile can be considered an educator's roadmap for guiding students' development of self-regulation.

Teacher

Instructs

Explicit Instruction of ALL Components (Instructional Criteria 1–3)

| Component 1 | Component 2 | Component 3 | Component 4 |

Make a Plan

- What do I need to accomplish by when?
- What are the steps?
- What could go wrong?
- How will I keep on track?

Monitor Your Plan

- Am I progressing as planned?
- What is or isn't working?
- What steps do I need to add or adjust?

Adjust as Needed

- What do I need to do to get back on track?
- What resources (including people) can I use to get back on track?

Reflect

- Is my plan effective?
- What should I apply to future efforts?

Student

Practices (Instructional Criteria 4 and 6)

Ongoing and fluid

Teacher

Coaches (Instructional Criteria 5)

- Reteach as needed (Instructional Criteria 1–3).
- Prompt students to consider previous self-regulation efforts.
- Review students' plans.
- Provide feedback on plans.
- Question and prompt.

- Prompt monitoring.
- Monitor the students' monitoring.
- Coach students to assess progress.

- Provide time to think through changes and edit plan.
- Coach students who are not making progress.
- Highlight and recognize when students are making changes.

- Facilitate *fluid* reflection—as students monitor and edit their plan.
- Prompt culminating reflection on strengths and areas for improvement.

Source: © 2016 by Amy Gaumer Erickson and Patricia Noonan. Used with permission.

FIGURE E.2: TEACHER AND STUDENT ROLES IN SELF-REGULATION INSTRUCTION.

Visit go.SolutionTree.com/SEL for a free reproducible version of this figure.

In the first domain, Preparing to Provide Instruction, we consider, as teachers, how well we understand the self-regulation components, vocabulary, and our ability to teach key concepts, and we create a plan for how we will deliver instruction to our students. The second domain, Providing Competency Instruction, addresses instructional criteria 1–3 (see figure E.1, page 144), including guiding students to personalize their new learning by identifying strengths and areas for growth. The third domain, Facilitating Practice with Feedback, guides us to consider how we are moving beyond teacher-directed instruction into facilitating guided and independent practice while supporting students to self-appraise their growth. Finally, the fourth domain, Using Data for Decision Making, helps us consider the degree to which we are using relevant data to guide instruction and communicating with others in our school (for example, teachers, counselors, administrators) regarding student progress.

Competency Framework Practice Profile for Teachers			
Directions: Self-assess on key indicators of quality self-regulation instruction while reflecting on your instructional activities over the last quarter.			
A. Preparing to Provide Self-Regulation Instruction			
	Educator Practices	**Novice**	**Emerging**	**Proficient**
A1	Teacher: • Demonstrates understanding of self-regulation and key concepts of competency instruction (including four essential components).	Teacher demonstrates limited understanding of self-regulation components and other key concepts; inconsistently uses correct vocabulary.	Teacher describes self-regulation components accurately and consistently uses correct vocabulary. Teacher explains key concepts competently but without depth or clear examples.	Teacher demonstrates a clear understanding of self-regulation components with consistent vocabulary and creative examples and ideas. Teacher demonstrates thoughtful insight into the explanation and analysis of key concepts, including personal examples.
A2	Teacher: • Creates a plan describing how self-regulation instruction will be provided and how students will practice with feedback.	Teacher creates a plan to provide self-regulation instruction but does not address all learning targets.	Teacher creates a plan to provide self-regulation instruction that addresses all learning targets but does not incorporate methods to measure growth in knowledge or performance.	Teacher creates a detailed plan to provide self-regulation instruction and practice with feedback that clearly addresses all learning targets and includes methods to observe students' knowledge and performance.
Notes or examples:			

FIGURE E.3: COMPETENCY FRAMEWORK PRACTICE PROFILE FOR TEACHERS.

continued →

B. Providing Self-Regulation Instruction				
	Educator Practices	**Novice**	**Emerging**	**Proficient**
B1	Teacher: • Provides instruction, addressing each learning target for the competency, to facilitate students' understanding of self-regulation (Instructional Criterion 1).	Teacher incorporates self-regulation instructional activities to address a few of the learning targets.	Teacher incorporates instructional activities for most of the learning targets.	Teacher incorporates instructional activities to address each self-regulation learning target. Teacher reteaches key concepts as needed.
B2	Teacher: • Guides students to determine how self-regulation applies to them personally (Instructional Criterion 2). • Facilitates students' reflection on their strengths and challenges related to self-regulation (Instructional Criterion 3).	Teacher prompts (but does not facilitate) students' application of self-regulation or reflection on strengths and challenges related to self-regulation components.	Teacher facilitates at least one opportunity for students' personal application of self-regulation or reflection on strengths and challenges related to self-regulation components.	Teacher facilitates students' ongoing, personal application of self-regulation and reflection on strengths and challenges related to the four self-regulation components.
Notes or examples:				

C. Facilitating Self-Regulation Practice With Feedback				
	Educator Practices	**Novice**	**Emerging**	**Proficient**
C1	Teacher: • Facilitates opportunities for students to practice self-regulation, including each component, over time (Instructional Criterion 4).	Teacher expresses an expectation that students demonstrate self-regulation and may provide group practice opportunities but does not facilitate students' individual practice in authentic settings.	Teacher provides classroom practice opportunities for each student that are infrequent (less than once per quarter) or address some (but not all) self-regulation components.	Teacher utilizes existing classroom curricula and activities to create authentic opportunities for each student to practice self-regulation, including each component, at least once per quarter. Practice is ongoing across multiple class sessions.
C2	Teacher: • Provides feedback to students throughout their practice of the self-regulation components (Instructional Criterion 5).	Teacher gives general feedback that does not address specific self-regulation components and is not provided to each student.	Teacher gives specific feedback throughout student practice but either does not address all four self-regulation components or does not reach all students.	Teacher gives specific feedback to each student regarding each self-regulation component, throughout and after student practice.

C3	Teacher: • Facilitates students' reflection on their development of self-regulation components (Instructional Criterion 6).	Teacher facilitates reflection on self-regulation development for a limited number of students or does not include all four components in reflection efforts.	Teacher facilitates reflection on self-regulation development for all students, but infrequently (for example, once per semester), and does not consistently address all four components.	Teacher facilitates reflection on development of all four self-regulation components at least quarterly for all students. Teacher guides students in identifying their personal growth in self-regulation concepts.
Notes or examples:				

D. Using Data for Decision Making

	Educator Practices	Novice	Emerging	Proficient
D1	Teacher: • Determines next steps in self-regulation instruction through data-based decision making.	Teacher collects limited data to assess students' self-regulation development and outcomes. Teacher does not use collected data to identify specific needs for additional instruction or student supports.	Teacher collects data regularly on students' self-regulation development and outcomes but does not consistently use data to guide decisions about future needs for instruction or supports.	Teacher follows an established plan for routinely collecting and analyzing data on students' self-regulation development and outcomes (such as pre- and post- knowledge, performance-based assessments, and school data points). Teacher uses the data to identify and implement additional instruction and supports for students.
D2	Teacher: • Collaborates with others on a regular basis to enhance self-regulation instruction.	Teacher works in isolation, rarely discussing self-regulation instructional ideas with others.	Teacher collaborates with colleagues occasionally but does not consistently seek or provide instructional ideas and feedback.	Teacher has a well-established process for collaboration, which includes regularly requesting and sharing feedback and instructional ideas with colleagues.
Notes or examples:				

The Competency Framework Practice Profile for Teachers (figure E.3, page 147) is completed periodically by individual teachers who are implementing self-regulation instruction to self-assess their degree of implementation and identify areas for growth in instruction. When used schoolwide, teachers throughout the building self-assess and work with peers to better meet instructional objectives and promote student growth.

WHAT TEACHERS SAY

"It's not just about kids; as teachers, we developed this collective teacher efficacy, and we became a team. That is one of the things that I think using the framework did for the school that was just really darn amazing."

—Vickie, language arts teacher

Schoolwide Tier 1 Implementation

When it comes to the development of intrapersonal competencies like self-regulation, educators have each historically worked in isolation. Impact on students can be far greater through collaboration across roles, between content areas, and even beyond the school. In our work supporting thousands of teachers in providing self-regulation instruction, it is clear that schoolwide Tier 1 instruction results in stronger application and improved student outcomes as opposed to educators working in isolation or with only students demonstrating the greatest need. In many states, priorities for social-emotional learning have emerged as critical for student success, taking the form of standards, individual plans of study, statewide initiatives, and school board priorities. To this end, many schools are adopting SEL curricula and interventions. An assembly of activities in this book, taught systematically while measuring student growth, provides the foundation for a Tier 1, evidence-based, SEL curriculum. Beyond the activities outlined in the prior chapters, educators must design opportunities for students to continue practicing the self-regulation components.

Families should also be approached as partners in social-emotional development for their youth. By the high school level, families may not be able to support their children in learning advanced mathematics or science content, but they continue to be the primary guides for their children's development of intrapersonal and interpersonal skills. Like educators, families can learn and apply the self-regulation concepts to their own lives and promote practice opportunities for their children. Families can prompt and coach their children to self-regulate as well as listen and ask questions when adjustments are needed. Through ongoing collaboration with families and community members, a community-wide vision can guide ongoing efforts to promote the success of each youth.

WHAT TEACHERS SAY

"It was neat to be able to go from classroom to classroom and see how self-regulation was being taught and applied to different situations that came up due to student questions. The difference for me [from other SEL curricula] was to be able to see the meaningful discussions happen and see how students were able to talk about how they were going to apply this."

—*James, high school principal*

When middle and high schools adopt self-regulation as an SEL curriculum, teachers, counselors, special educators, related service providers, and administrators all learn self-regulation instructional practices, often through ongoing professional development and coaching. All educators, regardless of their role, learn how to teach self-regulation and provide practice with feedback to students. Self-regulation is also incorporated into other initiatives and systems, such as schoolwide disciplinary protocols or behavior expectations. All students (including those identified as gifted, with disabilities, at risk, or on track) benefit from this instruction.

In addition to explicit instruction schoolwide, data-based decision making supports self-regulation efforts as data are gathered, interpreted, and shared to understand trends and inform important decisions. In this process, educators, administrators, and other stakeholders use data to collaboratively set goals and create plans to enact change and monitor progress. Data guide improvements at all levels of the education system, from data regarding the instructional needs for a single student to schoolwide data that inform Tier I, universal instruction.

WHAT TEACHERS SAY

"All the teachers were using the same vocabulary in their other classes, so the students had multiple opportunities for exposure. Across classes, students were guided to use the process."

—*Eve, assistant principal*

When schools decide to teach all students how to better self-regulate, the first step is to develop a clear path for all educators to learn, implement, and scale-up instruction. Administrators support teachers in planning and delivering quality instruction, collecting and analyzing data, overcoming challenges, and reflecting on the impact of instruction (such as through professional learning, instructional coaching, and ongoing collaboration). Administrators also teach and reinforce self-regulation in their interactions with students. Teachers facilitate learning and then reflect and communicate with each other to determine successes and overcome barriers. Instruction and practice are then systematized into ongoing classroom activities, becoming a standard way of work and a part of daily school life. Self-regulation becomes fully embedded in school culture, and parents and community members are aware of and included in a common vision.

Summary

This book supports teachers in learning how to provide self-regulation instruction and practice opportunities within middle and high schools. You are joining educators from around the world in expanding social-emotional learning. Your self-regulation instruction will improve with your efforts over time—remember, just like students, you too will improve through numerous opportunities to practice. Our vision is to increase each educator's capacity to foster growth in self-regulation to create a society of socially and emotionally engaged, career-equipped, lifelong learners.

APPENDIX A

SITUATIONAL JUDGMENT ASSESSMENT

Situational Judgment Assessment

Based on the scenario and what you know about self-regulation, answer each prompt.

SCENARIO

In health class, Alex and his classmates learned about the benefits of drinking an adequate amount of water each day. Alex has decided that he does not drink enough water.

Activity 9

Write three questions that Alex should ask himself to become more aware of his water consumption and behaviors that he may need to change in order to meet his goal of drinking an adequate amount of water each day.

Activity 23

Make a five-step daily plan for Alex that will result in his increased water consumption. Assume that Alex goes to your school and participates in the same classes and extracurricular activities as you.

Activity 37

Determine when and how Alex will monitor his progress and actions throughout each day.

Activity 50

Write three if–then statements that address obstacles Alex is likely to encounter.

Activity 61

Write three questions that Alex could use to guide his reflection. Identify when and how Alex will reflect on his progress and actions.

Activity 72

Review the plan that you developed for Alex to drink more water. Now that you know more about the importance of all four self-regulation components, what would you add to his plan?

Grading Guidance

Activity 9

Review each student's answers to determine whether the questions they identified would increase self-awareness. Questions might include: How much water do I drink each day? When do I drink water? What do I drink instead of water? How much water should I be drinking each day? Why don't I drink more water (it's not available or I don't like the taste)? Provide specific, constructive feedback to each student.

Activity 23

Review each student's answers to determine whether the steps identified would likely increase Alex's water intake. Were five distinct steps identified? Which common planning elements (see figure 2.3, page 41) are included? Do the steps address obstacles such as not having water with you? Is a monitoring method included in the plan? Provide specific, constructive feedback to each student.

Activity 37

Review each student's answers to determine whether the monitoring methods include both progress (water consumption) and numerous actions (such as bringing water to school or drinking water at key intervals throughout the day).

Activity 50

Review each student's answer to determine whether the if-then statements address barriers that would likely impact Alex's water consumption. Examples might include the following.

- If I forget my water at home, then I'll buy one from the vending machine.

- If I haven't drunk enough water before lunch, then I'll finish what's in my water bottle before I start eating.

- If I don't like the taste of the water at school, then I'll keep liquid flavoring in my backpack.

Activity 61

Review each student's answers to determine whether the reflection occurs at frequent intervals and goes beyond monitoring. Example questions might include the following.

- How is my water consumption impacting the way I feel?

- On days when I drink enough water, what am I doing to be successful at this?

- On days when I don't drink enough water, what am I missing or forgetting to do?

- Overall, is my health improving by increasing my water consumption?

Alex could reflect daily using a log.

Activity 72

Analyze each student's response looking for detailed description for improving planning, monitoring, adjusting, and reflecting. Provide specific, constructive feedback to each student.

SELF-REGULATION QUESTIONNAIRE AND KNOWLEDGE TEST

Self-Regulation Questionnaire and Knowledge Test

SELF-REGULATION QUESTIONNAIRE

Student ID _____   **Date** _____

Please check one response that best describes you. The information will be used to help you reflect on your strengths and areas for growth. There are no right or wrong answers!

	Not very like me ⟵ ⟶ Very like me				
	1	2	3	4	5
1. I plan out projects that I want to complete.	☐	☐	☐	☐	☐
2. If an important test is coming up, I create a study plan.	☐	☐	☐	☐	☐
3. Before I do something fun, I consider all the things that I need to get done.	☐	☐	☐	☐	☐
4. I can usually estimate how much time my homework will take to complete.	☐	☐	☐	☐	☐
5. It is hard for me to get started on a big assignment.	☐	☐	☐	☐	☐
6. I have trouble making plans to help me reach my goals.	☐	☐	☐	☐	☐
7. I keep track of how my projects are going.	☐	☐	☐	☐	☐
8. I know when I'm behind on a project.	☐	☐	☐	☐	☐
9. I track my progress for reaching my goal.	☐	☐	☐	☐	☐
10. I know what my grades are at any given time.	☐	☐	☐	☐	☐
11. Daily, I identify things I need to get done and track what gets done.	☐	☐	☐	☐	☐
12. I often lose track of time.	☐	☐	☐	☐	☐
13. I have trouble remembering all the things I need to accomplish.	☐	☐	☐	☐	☐
14. I do what it takes to get my homework done on time.	☐	☐	☐	☐	☐
15. I make choices to help me succeed, even when they aren't the most fun right now.	☐	☐	☐	☐	☐
16. As soon as I see things aren't going right, I want to do something about it.	☐	☐	☐	☐	☐

	Not very like me ◄————► Very like me				
	1	2	3	4	5
17. I keep trying as many different possibilities as necessary to succeed.	☐	☐	☐	☐	☐
18. When I want something expensive, I cut down on buying small things to save money for it.	☐	☐	☐	☐	☐
19. My friends can talk me into things that I later regret.	☐	☐	☐	☐	☐
20. I have difficulty maintaining my focus on projects that take a long time to complete.	☐	☐	☐	☐	☐
21. When I get behind on my work, I often give up.	☐	☐	☐	☐	☐
22. I think about how well I'm doing on my assignments.	☐	☐	☐	☐	☐
23. I feel a sense of accomplishment when I get everything done on time.	☐	☐	☐	☐	☐
24. I think about how well I've done in the past when I set new goals.	☐	☐	☐	☐	☐
25. When I'm criticized, I consider what I could have done differently.	☐	☐	☐	☐	☐
26. When I fail at something, I try to learn from my mistakes.	☐	☐	☐	☐	☐
27. When I've been struggling with something, I don't want to think about it.	☐	☐	☐	☐	☐
28. I keep making the same mistakes over and over again.	☐	☐	☐	☐	☐

Source: © 2019 by Amy Gaumer Erickson and Patricia Noonan. Used with permission.

SELF-REGULATION KNOWLEDGE TEST

Select the best answer.

29. Choose the best description of self-regulation.

   a. When you proactively plan for how to reach a goal, learn a skill, or accomplish a task

   b. When you proactively use a process (such as planning, monitoring the plan, making changes as needed, and reflecting) to reach a goal, learn a skill, or accomplish a task

   c. When you follow your teacher's detailed directions (including making changes as suggested by your teacher and reflecting on your progress) for reaching a goal, learning a skill, or accomplishing a task

   d. When you make progress toward reaching a goal, learning a skill, or accomplishing a task

Decide if each of the following scenarios describes at least one component of self-regulation.	
Scenario	**Is it self-regulation?**
30. After school, your parent takes your phone and says you'll get it back when your homework is done.	Yes No
31. You want to improve your grade in English, so you check your grade every Friday to see if it has gotten better.	Yes No
32. You write down the homework that you need to complete and check it off your list as you finish it, making sure to finish each assignment.	Yes No
33. You were working on your mathematics assignment and came to a problem that you didn't know how to solve. You texted your friend for help, but he hasn't responded, so you leave the answer blank.	Yes No
34. Which of these things is NOT likely to be a result of improving your self-regulation? a. Increased control of your learning and academic success b. Increased ability to recognize and address your own mistakes c. Increased ability to reach goals without encountering any barriers d. Improved time management and organization	
35. Identify the best example of using the self-regulation process to address problems with being late to school. a. Telling a parent or guardian about the problem and asking for help to get you to school on time b. Setting an extra alarm tomorrow to make it more likely that you will get up on time; that should eliminate the problem c. Considering possible reasons for your tardiness (such as staying up too late or not gathering supplies until morning) and making a plan to address those things, including how to see if you're making progress d. Deciding that now that you're aware of the issue, you won't have trouble tomorrow—you know you just need to get up with the alarm, instead of hitting snooze or turning it off; then you won't be late	

Identify which self-regulation component (plan, monitor, make changes, reflect) each behavior addresses.	
Behavior	**Component**
36. Each day, crossing tasks off a to-do list as you finish them	Plan Monitor Adjust Reflect
37. Recognizing when something isn't working and immediately adjusting your actions to get back on track	Plan Monitor Adjust Reflect
38. Thinking each day about successes, setbacks, and specific things you've learned	Plan Monitor Adjust Reflect
39. Breaking down big goals into smaller pieces	Plan Monitor Adjust Reflect
40. After encountering setbacks, looking for solutions and trying as many as needed	Plan Monitor Adjust Reflect
41. Thinking about your past efforts when setting new goals	Plan Monitor Adjust Reflect
42. Using specific ways to track your progress	Plan Monitor Adjust Reflect

43. Which of these actions does not specifically address a self-regulation component?

    a. Creating a study plan for important tests or a timeline of tasks or steps for long-term projects

    b. Checking your grades every week to see how teachers have graded your performance on assignments, projects, and tests

    c. Knowing when you are behind on a task and figuring out the best steps to take to get back on track

    d. Having specific methods in mind for how you will measure your progress as you work toward a goal

44. Which of these would you NOT use to monitor progress on your self-regulation plan?

    a. A graph showing your progress over time

    b. A journal where you describe daily progress and identify if you are on track with on your plan

    c. A rubric to compare with your work to see if you are meeting the criteria

    d. A comparison of your progress to your friend's progress on the same project or assignment

45. You are told to write an essay, due in three weeks. The last time you had a task like this, you didn't write it until the night before. Your grade wasn't very good, and you want to do better. Using what you've learned, choose the best option.

    a. Break the assignment down into the basic parts (for example, choose a topic, outline the essay, write the essay, and so on), and estimate how much time each part takes. Work backward to identify deadlines for each part. Afterward, reflect on the quality of your work.

    b. Talk about the project with your friend Beth, who is great at planning how to space out work. Ask her what her timeline is for accomplishing the project, and make that your timeline, too. After you finish, reflect on how well you did.

    c. See your teacher to discuss your difficulties with this type of assignment and ask what you should do differently this time. Follow the teacher's plan and timeline to complete each part of the assignment, getting back on track when necessary.

    d. Break the assignment down into the basic parts and make a plan for each part. Note specific tasks and their deadlines. Check off tasks as completed. If behind, figure out how to get back on track. During and after, consider what works and what could be improved.

Determine whether each statement is true or false.

46. _____ Self-regulation is important for academics, but it doesn't really help improve athletic or musical ability.

47. _____ Building your self-regulation skills can also help improve your goal-setting abilities.

48. _____ Using self-regulation can help you resist distractions.

_____

49. Imagine that you are struggling to learn a concept in mathematics. Provide brief descriptions of how you would address the first two components of self-regulation to work toward improving your learning.

    • Plan:

    • Monitor:

Source: © 2019 by Amy Gaumer Erickson and Patricia Noonan. Used with permission.

Answer Key

Questionnaire interpretation guidance: Items 5, 6, 12, 13, 19, 20, 21, 27, and 28 are negatively worded, meaning that lower ratings represent positive behaviors. When calculating averages, these items should be reversed scored.

Answer key for the knowledge test items: (29) B; (30) no; (31) no; (32) yes; (33) no; (34) C; (35) C; (36) monitor; (37) adjust; (38) reflect; (39) plan; (40) adjust; (41) reflect; (42) monitor; (43) B; (44) D; (45) D; (46) false; (47) true; and (48) true

APPENDIX C

SCENARIOS

Activity 19: Ava Wants More Energy—Planning for Healthy Eating;

Activity 58: Ava Reflects on Her Energy; and

Activity 69: The Impact of Missing Components on Ava's Energy

Ava lacks energy and spends too much money on energy drinks and cookies (her daily lunch). She falls asleep every afternoon in algebra and doesn't feel well in general. She wants to eat healthier. She decides to change her diet to low-sugar, minimally processed food, and shift to eating more protein, fruits, and vegetables. She gives away all her energy drinks and writes out a menu of what she will eat for breakfast, lunch, dinner, and snacks (using a nutritional guidance website to make sure that her menus will help her meet her goals). She discusses the plan with her family and asks her mom to stop buying cookies. She then records her food intake using an app. She gets off track at a weekend party, eating chips and cookies. The next day, she decides to keep granola bars and dried fruit in her purse so that she has an alternative to chips and cookies when at parties. Each day she reviews the data in the app, tracking nutrients consumed in relation to recommended daily allowances, and thinks about whether she ate a balanced diet that followed her menu. Using a printed calendar, Ava gives herself one to five stars for her effort that day and writes one personal success or challenge she experienced. Weekly, she thinks about what is working and what isn't, and then she revises her plan accordingly. She now has much more energy, stays awake in algebra, and feels healthier overall.

Activity 20: Anthony Wants to Save Money—Budgeting; and

Activity 34: Is Anthony Saving Money?

Anthony wants to save money for a gaming system. He has a part-time job and makes about $80 per week. Anthony usually spends all his money going out to eat with friends. Anthony knows that he's going to need to use self-regulation to save the money for the gaming system.

Activity 46: Anthony Gets Off Track While Saving Money

Anthony is trying to save money for a gaming system. He has a part-time job and makes about $80 per week. Following his plan, Anthony has started hanging out with friends at their houses and is going out to eat far less. This is working to save money. However, during breaks at work, Anthony is buying snacks and a soda from the vending machine. He hadn't thought about this when he made his plan, but these snacks are cutting into his savings. How can Anthony adjust his plan?

Activity 21: Olivia Needs a Homework Plan—Planning for Academic Success

Your younger sister, Olivia, who is in sixth grade, has been having trouble finishing her homework. She knows that lately you've been doing a lot better at turning things in on time, so she asks you to help her figure out how she can improve. You've been using self-regulation to increase your success, and you know that, in general, students who use self-regulation are more likely to complete their homework on time. You decide that the best way to support your sister is by helping her brainstorm a self-regulation plan for her homework completion.

Activity 35: Monitoring Olivia's Homework Plan

Olivia has been using the self-regulation plan for homework completion for two weeks now. She has been doing some monitoring. She checks off assignments that she turned in on time, and she uses the list to calculate her percentage of on-time homework—she is at 80 percent now, up from 50 percent before the plan. She can tell from comparing her first percentage to her current one that she has improved a lot, but she wants to improve further. The problem is that Olivia is not sure where she is getting off track, so she is asking you to help her figure it out. You know that to do this, she will have to expand her focus from just monitoring her percentage of assignments completed on time to include monitoring specific actions, so you decide to help her brainstorm how to expand her monitoring.

Activity 22: Levi's Anxiety Over Public Speaking—Strategies for Physiological Reactions

Your friend Levi is taking a public speaking class. He knows that he will be expected to speak in front of groups in the career he plans to pursue. The only problem is that Levi gets very anxious when speaking in front of a group. His palms sweat and his mouth gets very dry. He ends up talking too fast and without emotion. Help Levi make a plan for reducing his anxiety and effectively conveying his ideas to a group.

Activity 36: Is Levi's Anxiety Decreasing?

Your friend, Levi, is taking a public speaking class. He knows that he will be expected to speak in front of groups in the career he plans to pursue. The only problem is that Levi gets very anxious when speaking in front of a group. His palms sweat and his mouth gets very dry. He ends up talking too fast and without emotion. Help Levi monitor his plan for reducing his anxiety and effectively conveying his ideas to a group.

Activity 59: Reflecting on Levi's Public Speaking

Your friend Levi is taking a public speaking class. He knows that he will be expected to speak in front of groups in the career he plans to pursue. The only problem is that Levi gets very anxious when speaking in front of a group. His palms sweat and his mouth gets very dry. He ends up talking too fast and without emotion. Levi made a plan for feeling confident and reducing his anxiety when giving a speech. He followed this plan, which included practicing the speech many times in front of family, taking deep breaths before each practice speech, pausing in the middle to remember to speak slowly and with emotion, and repeating the phrase, "I am prepared for the speech. I can do this!" Yesterday, Levi gave his speech. Since it is a public speaking class, another speech has already been assigned. What should Levi think about when making his plan to master his next speech?

Activity 60: Preparing for a Capstone Project

To graduate, you must successfully complete a capstone project that demonstrates your knowledge and skill. It is expected that the project will take about six months for you to complete and will include research, a portfolio outlining your process, and a final product that demonstrates your achievement. How might you reflect on your strengths and past challenges as you prepare to take on this project?

Activity 70: Elijah Studies for an Exam

Elijah wants to get a B on his biology final. Per Elijah, "I'll create a study schedule, I'll complete two sections of the study guide each night, and I'll finish the study guide in five days. While I fill out the study guide, I'll make flash cards for any vocabulary terms that I don't already know. Next, I'll review all my previous tests from the semester and correct the answers I got wrong. I'll also quiz myself on all the vocabulary terms. Finally, I'll review all the diagrams for each concept, and I'll write down any questions I have and ask my friend Liam, who is amazing at biology, to explain anything I don't understand. I've got a plan, so I think I'll do well on the final."

After two days, Elijah reviewed his plan and checked on how he was doing: "Well, I only got one section of the study guide done, and I didn't write any vocabulary cards (because I don't have any index cards) for the section I did. I need to make some changes. I'll buy a pack of index cards from the school store before I go home today. I'll review the section that I did do for any vocabulary terms. I'll create flash cards for those terms. Next, to get caught up, I'll do all of sections 2 and 3 tonight and half of section 4. Tomorrow, I'll finish section 4 and do sections 5 and 6. I'll also make sure I keep up with the vocab flash cards. Then I'll be back on track."

STUDENT TEMPLATES

Project Plan and Log

Name of project:

Project due date:

Describe the project requirements:

Visualize success. What does it look like?

1. Make a plan

Think of all the tasks that are needed to complete this project, such as developing a timeline; gathering materials; learning the content (reading, viewing videos, talking to an expert or mentor); writing, editing, and revising drafts; creating a model or illustrations; checking your work against the project rubric; and so on.

Describe your plan to complete this project. Be specific!

Task	Date Due	Date Completed

page 1 of 3

Based on past experiences and obligations that you have coming up, what might go wrong with your plan? Describe how you will address the potential obstacles. Think about where and when you will work on the project, how you will avoid distractions, who you will go to if you need help, and so on.

Identify regular dates that you will monitor your plan, such as every Monday after school. List the dates and describe how you will remind yourself to monitor.

2. Monitor the plan (repeat for each monitoring date)

Am I meeting all of my deadlines? ☐ Yes ☐ No

Am I on track to complete the project on time? ☐ Yes ☐ No

If I answered *yes* to both questions, I should reflect by identifying what is helping me be successful, and continue doing that until the next time I monitor my plan. For example, doing a little work each night, reviewing my plan each day to make sure I stay on track, sharing my accomplishments with a friend, and so on.

What strategies are working well for me?

If I answered *no*, I need to figure out why my plan is not working.

What obstacles or challenges are preventing my plan from working?

☐ Time issues—too many other things are competing for my time.

☐ I am getting distracted when I work on the project.

☐ I am hung up on a certain step, specifically: _____

☐ I don't have a clear plan to begin with.

☐ I don't know what I need to do next.

☐ I don't understand the material or content enough to proceed.

☐ Other—specify: _____

3. Adjust as needed (repeat for each monitoring date)

What support do I need to get my plan back on track? What do I need to change to stay focused on my plan? My revised plan includes the following.

4. Reflect on what worked (do this when the project has been completed)

What went well? Be specific! For example, I stuck to my timeline, I used the project rubric as a guide, I reviewed and revised my work several times, I sought help from a teacher or knowledgeable peer, and so on.

What could I do differently on the next project to self-regulate?

Homework Log

Use this log to monitor your actions and progress for homework success. Reflect on the data to determine the accuracy of your predictions.

Planning					Monitoring Actions			Monitoring Progress	
Class and Assignment	Do I have all the materials?	Estimated difficulty (1 = Easy; 5 = Hard) Do I need help?	Do I need to break it into smaller pieces? If yes, add rows.	Estimated time needed to complete	Actual time to complete	Actual difficulty (1 = Easy; 5 = Hard)	Effort (1 = Low; 5 = High)	Anticipated grade	Actual grade

Source: © 2020 by Amy Gaumer Erickson and Patricia Noonan. Used with permission.

Teaching Self-Regulation © 2022 Solution Tree Press • SolutionTree.com

Visit **go.SolutionTree.com/SEL** to download this free reproducible.

Academic Success Plan and Log

Use this weekly plan and log to focus on your academic success. Remember to maintain the actions from the prior week as you determine a focus area for this week.

Week of: _____   Name: _____

Monday

Based on last week's academic success, this week I want to focus on the following.

☐ Completing and turning in homework

☐ Understanding course content

☐ Preparing for tests

☐ Participating in class

☐ Staying on track on projects

☐ Using class time wisely

☐ Turning in missing assignments

☐ Other: _____

Make a plan for improving the preceding item(s) checked (with specific steps, deadlines, things to monitor, ideas for overcoming potential barriers, and so on).

Tuesday	Wednesday	Thursday
Monitor the plan to determine how it's going. Am I doing what I said I would do? _____ Yes _____ No *If **yes**, I can continue what I am doing to be successful.* *If **no**, I need to figure out why I am not following my plan.* ☐ Time issues ☐ Didn't start with a clear plan ☐ Don't know what to do next ☐ Don't understand concept ☐ Other: _____	**Monitor the plan** to determine how it's going. Am I doing what I said I would do? _____ Yes _____ No *If **yes**, I can continue what I am doing to be successful.* *If **no**, I need to figure out why I am not following my plan.* ☐ Time issues ☐ Didn't start with a clear plan ☐ Don't know what to do next ☐ Don't understand concept ☐ Other: _____	**Monitor the plan** to determine how it's going. Am I doing what I said I would do? _____ Yes _____ No *If **yes**, I can continue what I am doing to be successful.* *If **no**, I need to figure out why I am not following my plan.* ☐ Time issues ☐ Didn't start with a clear plan ☐ Don't know what to do next ☐ Don't understand concept ☐ Other: _____

Tuesday	Wednesday	Thursday
Adjust my plan if needed:	**Adjust my plan** if needed:	**Adjust my plan** if needed:

Friday

Reflect on what worked and what could be improved by answering the following questions.

- What parts of your plan worked well for you?

- What parts of your plan could you change to be more effective next week?

- What do you need to do this weekend to stay on track (or get back on track)?

Feedback from teacher, mentor, or peer:

Source: © 2020 by Amy Gaumer Erickson and Patricia Noonan. Used with permission.

REFERENCES AND RESOURCES

American Educational Research Association, American Psychological Association, & National Council on Measurement in Education. (2014). *Standards for educational and psychological testing.* Washington, DC: American Educational Research Association.

BrainyQuote. (n.d.a). *Albert Einstein quotes.* Accessed at www.brainyquote.com /quotes/albert_einstein_106192 on May 11, 2021.

BrainyQuote. (n.d.b). *Michael Jordan quotes.* Accessed at www.brainyquote.com /quotes/michael_jordan_165967 on May 11, 2021.

BrainyQuote. (n.d.c). *Vince Lombardi quotes.* Accessed at https://www .brainyquote.com/authors/vince-lombardi-quotes on May 11, 2021.

Chen, P. P., & Bembenutty, H. (2018). Calibration of performance and academic delay of gratification: Individual and group differences in self-regulation of learning. In D. H. Schunk & J. A. Greene (Eds.), *Handbook of self-regulation of learning and performance* (2nd ed., pp. 407–420). New York: Routledge.

Cherry, K. (2020). *Famous quotes from American psychologist B. F. Skinner.* Accessed at www.verywellmind.com/b-f-skinner-quotes-2795688 on May 11, 2021.

Cleary, T. J., & Chen, P. P. (2009). Self-regulation, motivation, and math achievement in middle school: Variations across grade level and math context. *Journal of School Psychology, 47*(5), 291–314.

Cleary, T. J., & Zimmerman, B. J. (2012). A cyclical self-regulatory account of student engagement: Theoretical foundations and applications. In S. L. Christenson, A. L. Reschly, & C. Wylie (Eds.), *Handbook of research on student engagement* (pp. 237–257). New York: Springer.

Duckworth, A. L., Grant, H., Loew, B., Oettingen, G., & Gollwitzer, P. M. (2011). Self-regulation strategies improve self-discipline in adolescents: Benefits of mental contrasting and implementation intentions. *Educational Psychology, 31*(1), 17–26.

Duckworth, A. L., White, R. E., Matteucci, A. J., Shearer, A., & Gross, J. J. (2016). A stitch in time: Strategic self-control in high school and college students. *Journal of Educational Psychology, 108*(3), 329–341.

Frey, N., Hattie, J., & Fisher, D. (2018). *Developing assessment-capable visible learners, grades K–12: Maximizing skill, will, and thrill.* Thousand Oaks, CA: Corwin.

Gaumer Erickson, A. S., & Baird, K. (2019, November 11). *Beyond growth mindset: New frontiers in measuring engagement.* Paper presented at the National Literacy Summit, Orlando, FL.

Gaumer Erickson, A. S., & Noonan, P. M. (2015). *Research guide college and career competency: Self-regulation.* Accessed at http://researchcollaboration.org /uploads/ResearchGuide-Middle-High-Self-Regulation.pdf on October 18, 2021.

Gaumer Erickson, A. S., & Noonan, P. M. (2018). *College and career competency sequence preK–12: Self-regulation.* Accessed at http://cccframework.org/assets /sr-competencysequence.pdf on October 18, 2021.

Gaumer Erickson, A. S. & Noonan, P. M. (2019a). *Academic success tools.* Accessed at www.ResearchCollaboration.org/uploads/Academic-Success-Tools.pdf on October 18, 2021.

Gaumer Erickson, A. S., & Noonan, P. M. (2019b, September 11–12). *Challenges and strategies for implementing Tier I competency instruction in high schools.* Presented at the twelfth annual MTSS & Alignment Symposium, Wichita, KS.

Gaumer Erickson, A. S., & Noonan, P. M. (2021). *Self-regulation assessment suite.* Accessed at www.researchcollaborationsurveys.org/ on July 1, 2021.

Gaumer Erickson, A. S., Noonan, P. M., & Cooper, C. (2017). *Instructional criteria promotes progress to competence* [Infographic]. Accessed at www .ResearchCollaboration.org/uploads/Instructional-Criteria.pdf on October 18, 2021.

Gaumer Erickson, A. S., Noonan, P. M., & Monroe, K. A. (2020). *Self-regulation assessment suite: Technical report.* Accessed at http://researchcollaboration.org /uploads/Self-Regulation-Assess-Suite-Tech-2021.pdf on October 18, 2021.

Gaumer Erickson, A. S., Noonan, P. M., & Redeker, W. (2016). *Teacher and student roles in self-regulation* [Infographic]. Accessed at www.Research Collaboration.org/uploads/Teacher-Student-Roles-in-Self-Regulation -Instruction.pdf on October 18, 2021.

Ghanizadeh, A. (2017). The interplay between reflective thinking, critical thinking, self-monitoring, and academic achievement in higher education. *Higher Education, 74*(1), 101–114.

Gollwitzer, P. M. (1999). Implementation intentions: Strong effects of simple plans. *American Psychologist, 54*(7), 493–503.

Gollwitzer, A., Oettingen, G., Kirby, T. A., Duckworth, A. L., & Mayer, D. (2011). Mental contrasting facilitates academic performance in school children. *Motivation and Emotions, 35,* 403–412.

Goodreads. (n.d.a). *Antoine de Saint-Exupéry quotes.* Accessed at https://www .goodreads.com/quotes/87476-a-goal-without-a-plan-is-just-a-wish on May 11, 2021.

Goodreads. (n.d.b). *Maya Angelou quotes*. Accessed at www.goodreads.com /quotes/93512-you-may-encounter-many-defeats-but-you-must-not-be on May 11, 2021.

Guderjahn, L., Gold, A., Stadler, G., & Gawrilow, C. (2013). Self-regulation strategies support children with ADHD to overcome symptom-related behavior in the classroom. *Attention Deficit Hyperactivity Disorders, 5*(4), 397–407.

Guzman, G., Goldberg, T. S., & Swanson, H. L. (2018). A meta-analysis of self-monitoring on reading performance of K–12 students. *School Psychology Quarterly, 33*(1), 160–168.

Hadwin, A., Jarvela, S., & Miller, M. (2018). Self-regulation, co-regulation, and shared regulation in collaborative learning environments. In D. H. Schunk & J. A. Greene (Eds.), *Handbook of self-regulation of learning and performance* (2nd ed., pp. 83–106). New York: Routledge.

Harks, B., Rakoczy, K., Hattie, J., Besser, M., & Klieme, E. (2014). The effects of feedback on achievement, interest and self-evaluation: The role of feedback's perceived usefulness. *Educational Psychology, 34*(3), 269–290.

Hattie, J. (2009). *Visible learning: A synthesis of over 800 meta-analyses relating to achievement*. London: Routledge.

Hattie, J., & Zierer, K. (2018). *10 mindframes for visible learning: Teaching for success*. New York: Routledge.

Hoyle, R. H., & Dent, A. L. (2018). Developmental trajectories of skills and abilities relevant for self-regulation of learning and performance. In D. H. Schunk & J. A. Greene (Eds.), *Handbook of self-regulation of learning and performance* (2nd ed., pp. 49–63). New York: Routledge.

Ivcevic, Z., & Brackett, M. (2014). Predicting school success: Comparing conscientiousness, grit, and emotion regulation ability. *Journal of Research in Personality, 52*, 29–36.

Jiang, J., & Cameron, A. F. (2020). IT-enabled self-monitoring for chronic disease self-management: An interdisciplinary review. *MIS Quarterly, 44*(1), 451–508.

Kincaid, J. P., Fishburne, R. P., Rogers, R. L., & Chissom, B. S. (1975). *Derivation of new readability formulas (automated readability index, fog count, and Flesch reading ease formula) for Navy enlisted personnel*. Research Branch Report 8–75. Millington, TN: Naval Air Station Memphis.

Mallory, W. S. (2012). *I have gotten a lot of results! I know several thousand things that won't work*. Accessed at https://quoteinvestigator.com/2012/07/31/edison -lot-results/ on May 11, 2021.

Noonan, P. M., & Gaumer Erickson, A. S. (2018). *The skills that matter: Teaching interpersonal and intrapersonal competencies in any classroom*. Thousand Oaks, CA: Corwin.

Noonan, P. M., Gaumer Erickson, A. S., Heger, E., & Loewenstein, M. (2020). *Competency framework practice profile for teachers*. Accessed at www.Research Collaboration.org/uploads/Self-Regulation-Practice-Profile.pdf on October 18, 2021.

Oettingen, G. (2014). *Rethinking positive thinking: Inside the new science of motivation*. New York: Current.

Ramdass, D., & Zimmerman, B. J. (2011). Developing self-regulation skills: The important role of homework. *Journal of Advanced Academics*, *22*(2), 194–218.

Research Collaboration. (2020, November 6). *Clip 1: Izzy defines self-regulation* [Video]. Accessed at https://youtu.be/4KIeQUZDMWE on October 18, 2021.

Ritualize. (2017). *6 motivational quotes for inspiration.* Accessed at https://ritualize.com/5-motivational-health-quotes/ on August 23, 2021.

Santangelo, T., Harris, K. R., & Graham, S. (2016). Self-regulation and writing: Meta-analysis of the self-regulation processes in Zimmerman and Risemberg's model. In C. A. MacArthur, S. Graham, & J. Fitzgerald (Eds.), *Handbook of writing research* (2nd ed., pp.174–193). New York: Guilford Press.

Scholer, A. A., Ozaki, Y., & Higgins, E. T. (2014). Inflating and deflating the self: Sustaining motivational concerns through self-evaluation. *Journal of Experimental Social Psychology, 51,* 60–73.

Schunk, D. H., & Greene, J. A. (2018). Historical, contemporary, and future perspectives on self-regulated learning and performance. In D. H. Schunk & J. A. Greene (Eds.), *Handbook of self-regulation of learning and performance* (2nd ed., pp. 1–15). New York: Routledge.

Sentis. (2012, November 26). *Emotions and the brain* [Video]. Accessed at https://youtube.com/watch?v=xNY0AAUtH3g on October 18, 2021.

Usher, E. L., & Schunk, D. H. (2018). Social cognitive theoretical perspective of self-regulation. In D. H. Schunk & J. A. Greene (Eds.), *Handbook of self-regulation of learning and performance* (2nd ed., pp. 19–35). New York: Routledge.

White, M. C., & DiBenedetto, M. K. (2018). Self-regulation: An integral part of standards-based education. In D. H. Schunk & J. A. Greene (Eds.), *Handbook of self-regulation of learning and performance* (2nd ed., pp. 208–222). New York: Routledge.

Wilderotter, P. T. (2014). *Remembering Superman.* Accessed at www.christopherreeve.org/about-us/executive-memos/on-christopher-reeves-birthday on May 11, 2021.

Winne, P. H. (2018). Cognition and metacognition within self-regulated learning. In D. H. Schunk & J. A. Greene (Eds.), *Handbook of self-regulation of learning and performance* (2nd ed., pp. 36–48). New York: Routledge.

Yeager, D. S., Dahl, R. E., & Dweck, C. S. (2018). Why interventions to influence adolescent behavior often fail but could succeed. *Perspectives on Psychological Science, 13*(1), 101–122.

Zimmerman, B. J. (2013). From cognitive modeling to self-regulation: A social cognitive career path. *Educational Psychologist, 48*(3), 135–147.

Zimmerman, B. J., & Kitsantas, A. (2014). Comparing students' self-discipline and self-regulation measures and their prediction of academic achievement. *Contemporary Educational Psychology, 39*(2), 145–155.

INDEX

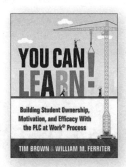

You Can Learn!
Tim Brown and William M. Ferriter
Great learning starts when students believe in their academic abilities. In _You Can Learn!_, authors Tim Brown and William M. Ferriter introduce intentional and purposeful steps your PLC team can take to increase the self-efficacy of every learner.
BKG020

Fifty Strategies to Boost Cognitive Engagement
Rebecca Stobaugh
Transform your classroom from one of passive knowledge consumption to one of active engagement. In this well-researched book, Rebecca Stobaugh shares 50 strategies for building a thinking culture that emphasizes essential 21st century skills—from critical thinking and problem-solving to teamwork and creativity.
BKF894

Problems-First Learning
Ted McCain
Discover a compelling alternative to traditional teaching practices: the problems-first instructional method. Using this method, you will fully engage students by first introducing a problem and then empowering learners to solve it using creativity, collaboration, and other essential skills.
BKF944

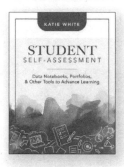

Student Self-Assessment
Katie White
Increase the achievement of every learner with _Student Self-Assessment_. In this practical guide, author Katie White outlines how to plan and implement various self-assessment strategies to ensure student growth at all grade levels. She covers every stage of the process—from setup to goal setting to celebrating.
BKG038

The Metacognitive Student: How to Teach Academic, Social, and
Richard K. Cohen, Deanne Kildare Opatosky, James Savage, Susan Olsen Stevens, and Edward P. Darrah
What if there was one strategy you could use to support students academically, socially, and emotionally? It exists—and it's simple, straightforward, and practical. Dive deep into structured SELf-questioning and learn how to empower students to develop into strong, healthy, and confident thinkers.
BKF954

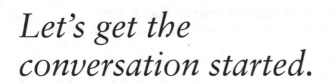